PREGNANCY COLORING BOOK
FOR ADULTS

RELAXING MANDALA DRAWINGS TO
HONOR MOTHERS AND BABIES

SILVIA SHAMUS &

MARC SHAMUS

iMasterLife.com

Edited by:

Marc Shamus

Illustrated by:

Silvia Shamus & Marc Shamus

Published by:

i Master Life Publishing

Pregnancy Coloring Book for Adults / Silvia Shamus & Marc Shamus
ISBN-13: 978-1-945719-07-3

CONTENTS

PERSONAL MESSAGE FROM SILVIA SHAMUS

Hi. Thank you so much for buying our book. This book is a resource that can help you to relax and de-stress from the day to day circumstances you face. Art activities like coloring help guide your focus away from these things to gain a different perspective. The unique pregnancy designs in this book will aid you to clear your mind, meditate and have fun.

Motherhood is such a precious and magical time. Both body and mind come together to create this sacred gift we call children. As parents of five children, my husband Marc & I know first hand how busy your day to day life can be. Some days you just need a break from the responsibilities; not just as parents, but as spouses. Depending on your work and lifestyle, a little "ME" time can come as a heavenly reward.

I loved pregnancy every time I went through it. I celebrated every aching and non aching moment. I remember having a lot of down time. Now you can have an activity that not only is fun, but has been proven to decrease stress. As you prepare for your child to be born, go back in time and remember when you were a child. Remember how fun it was to color and create art. Connect yourself with those memories.

You will really love these amazing pregnancy inspired illustrations! Fill in page after page as you bring Mandala style drawings to life with the colors of your choice. You can color with watercolor pencils, crayons, colored pencils, pastels, artist's markers or even watercolors. No matter what you use to color with, the final creations will be a sight for everyone to marvel at.

Have fun while clearing your mind. Relax and Rejuvenate from Stress Quickly with our Pregnancy Coloring Book. Get out your favorite color right now. Let your imagination run wild as you start to add your own style to each page. In fact, you may like what you color so much that you may use it in your own baby nursery or picture scrapbook. Enjoy!.

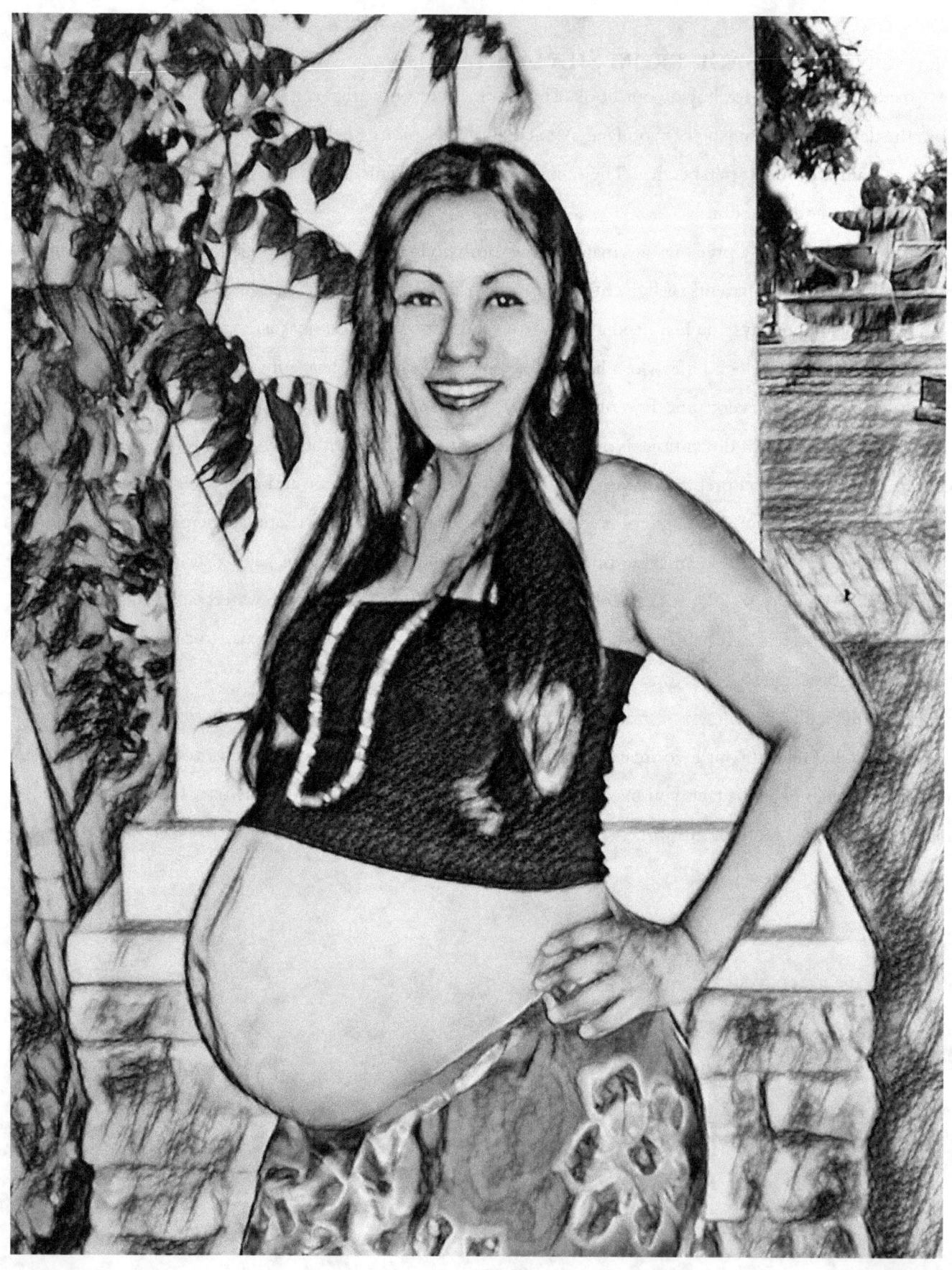

Silvia Shamus in September 2015 Pregnant with Fifth Baby

NOTE FROM THE PUBLISHER

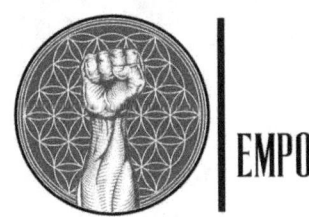

i Master Life
EMPOWERING . ENGAGING . TRANSFORMING

Thank you for purchasing this **i Master Life Publishing** book. Our goal is to get high quality <u>Life Mastery</u> materials and other worthwhile media into the hands of incredible people like you.

FOLLOW US:

Join our mailing list and get updates on new releases, deals, bonus content and other great publications from **i Master Life Publishing**.
iMasterLife.com/fan

SUPPORT US:

If you enjoyed this or any of our other books, would you please help support **I Master Life**. The sustainable revenue you provide ensures we can continue to provide publishing the very best media possible for you.

Just go to this link:
iMasterLife.com/fund

Thank You!

Marc

Marc A. Shamus
Founder

4

1. PACIFIER

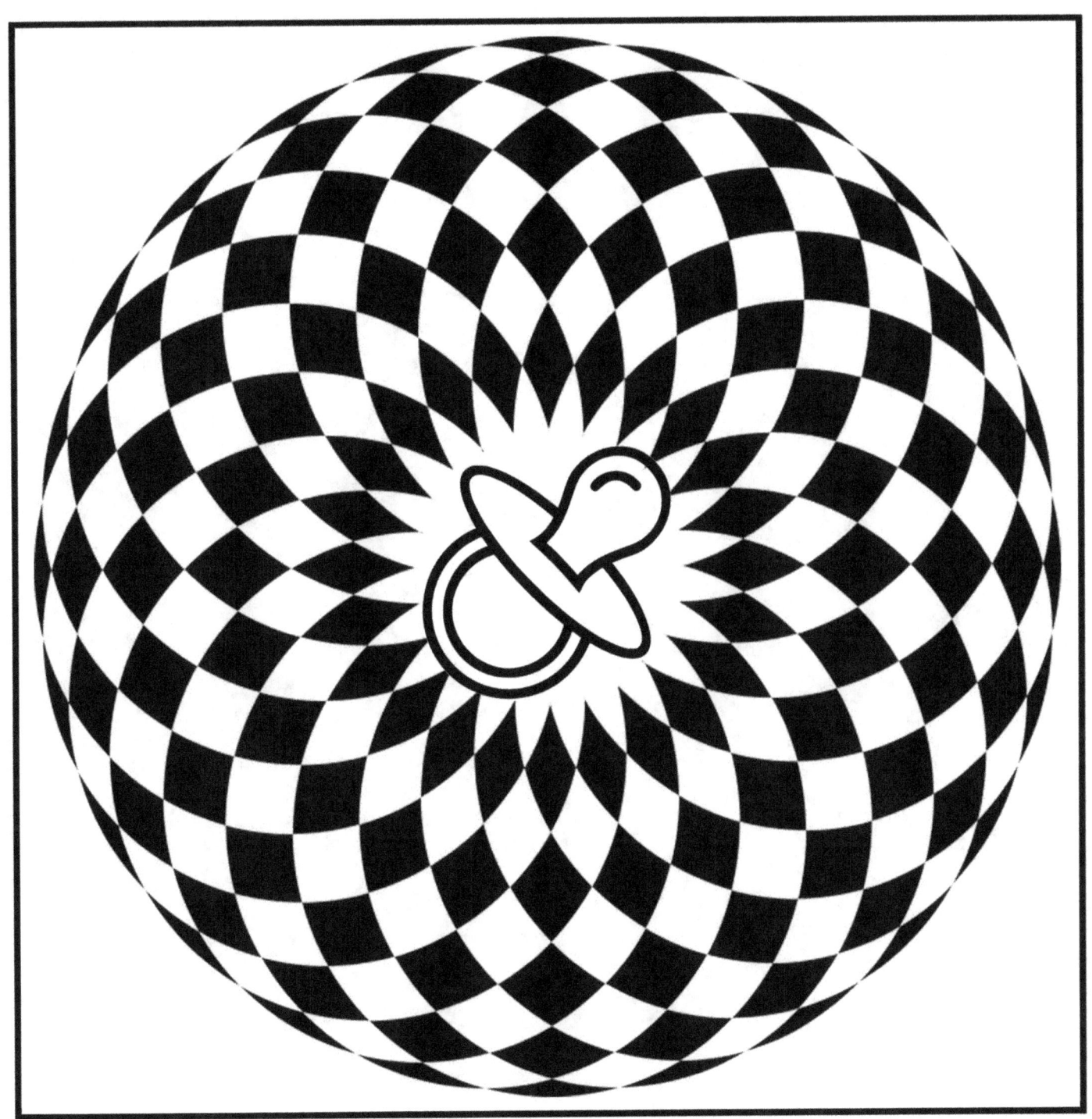

2. BABY SHOES

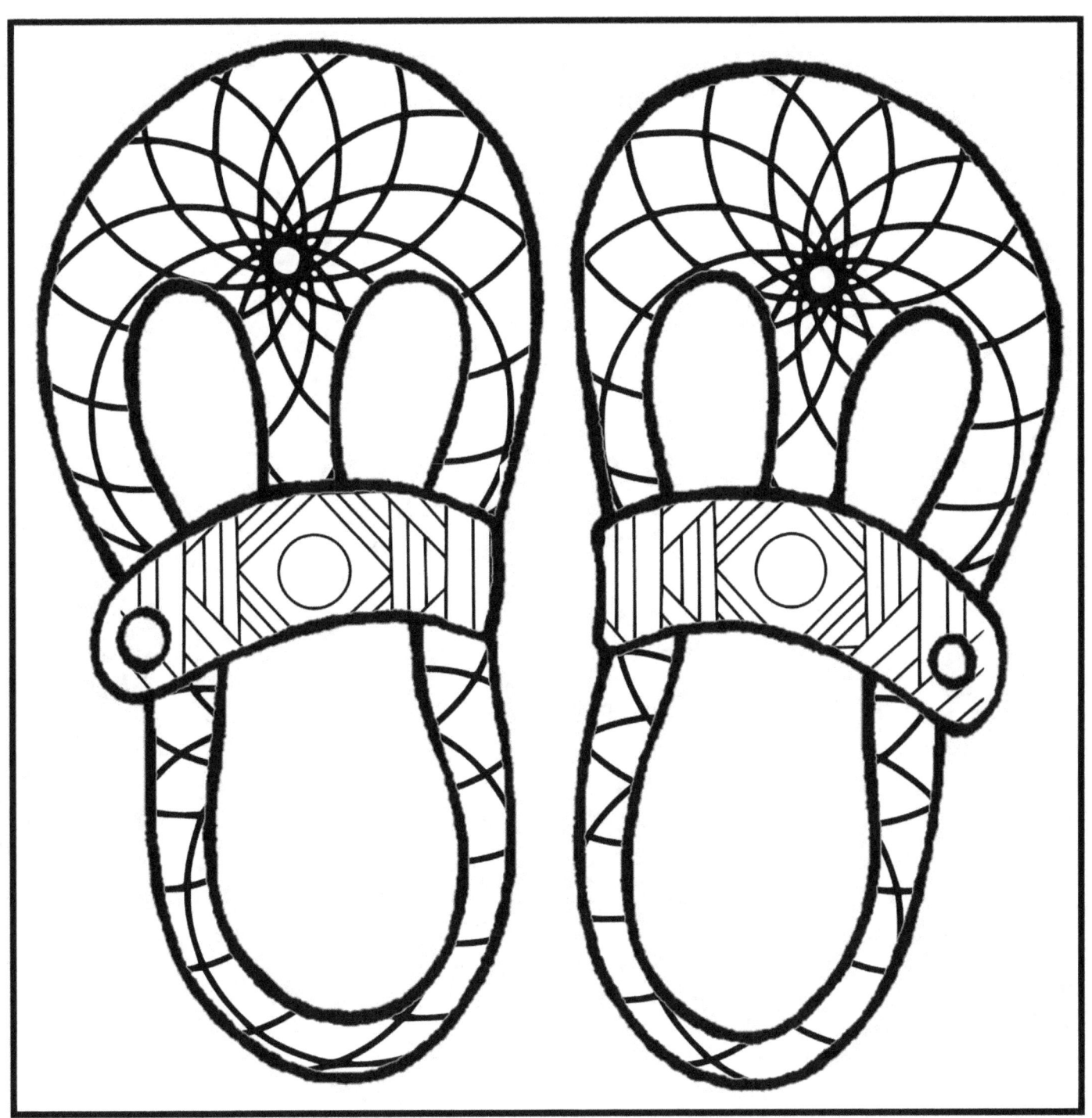

3. FETUS SUCKING HAND

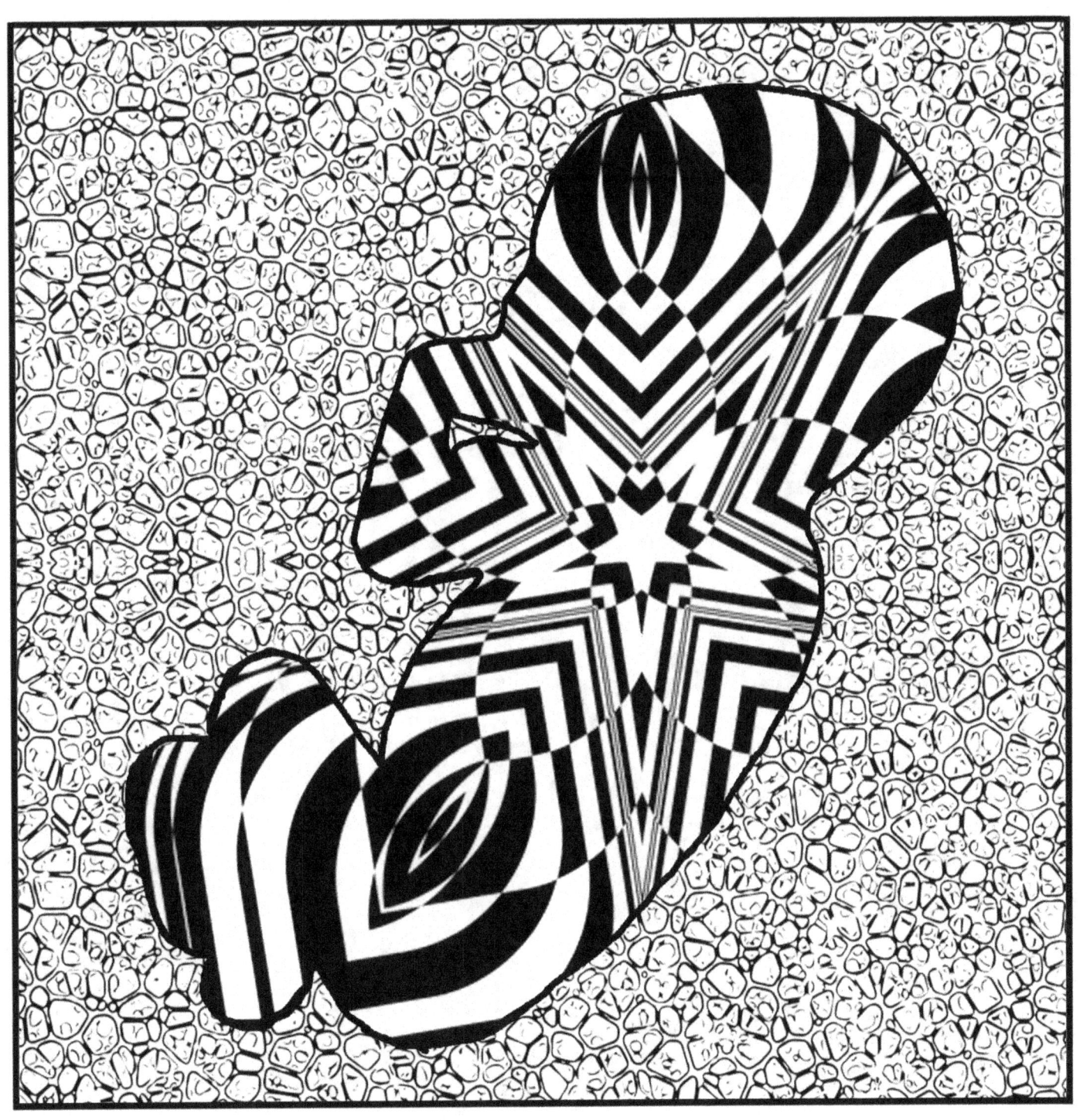

4. It's a Boy

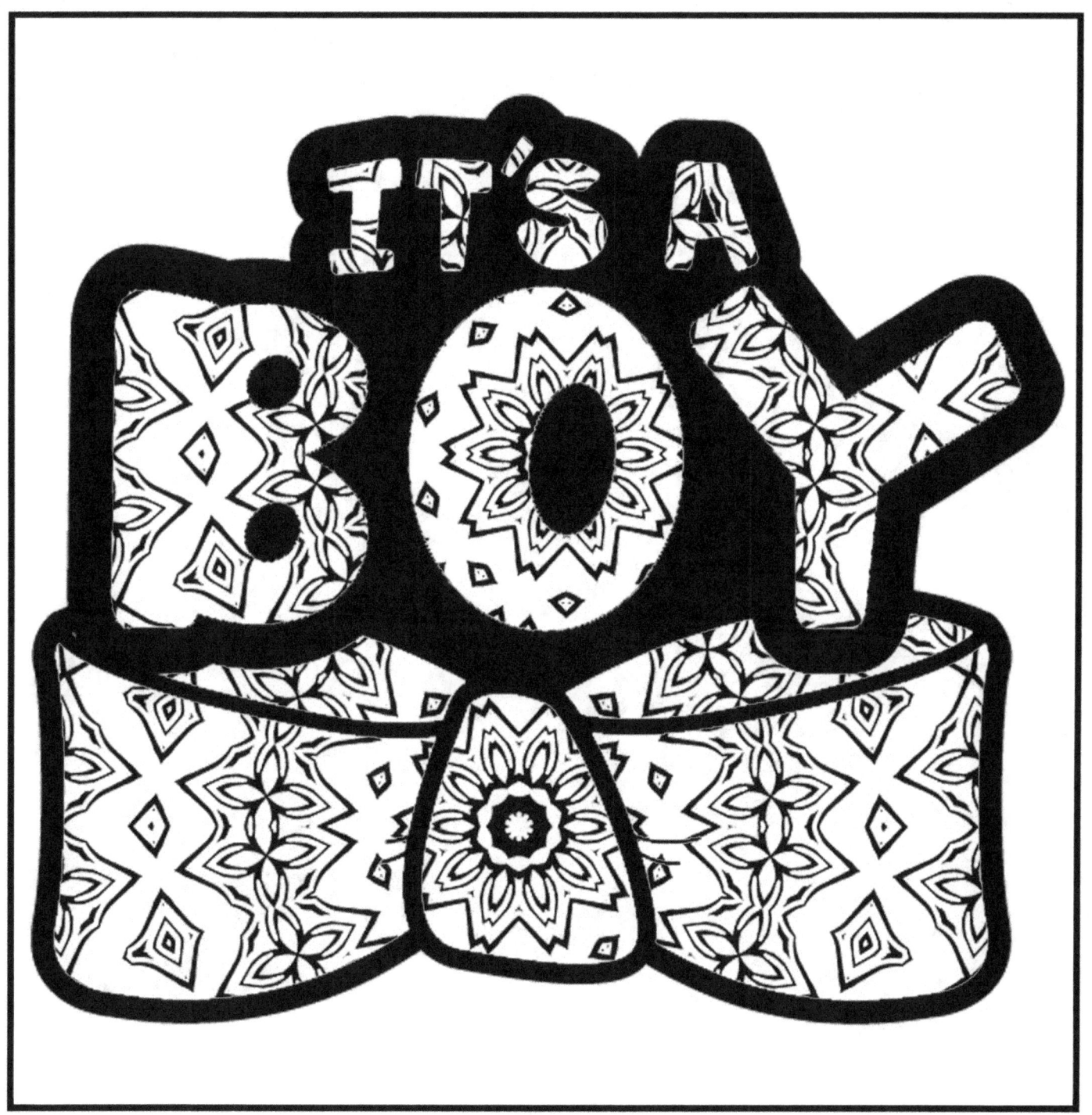

5. It's a Girl

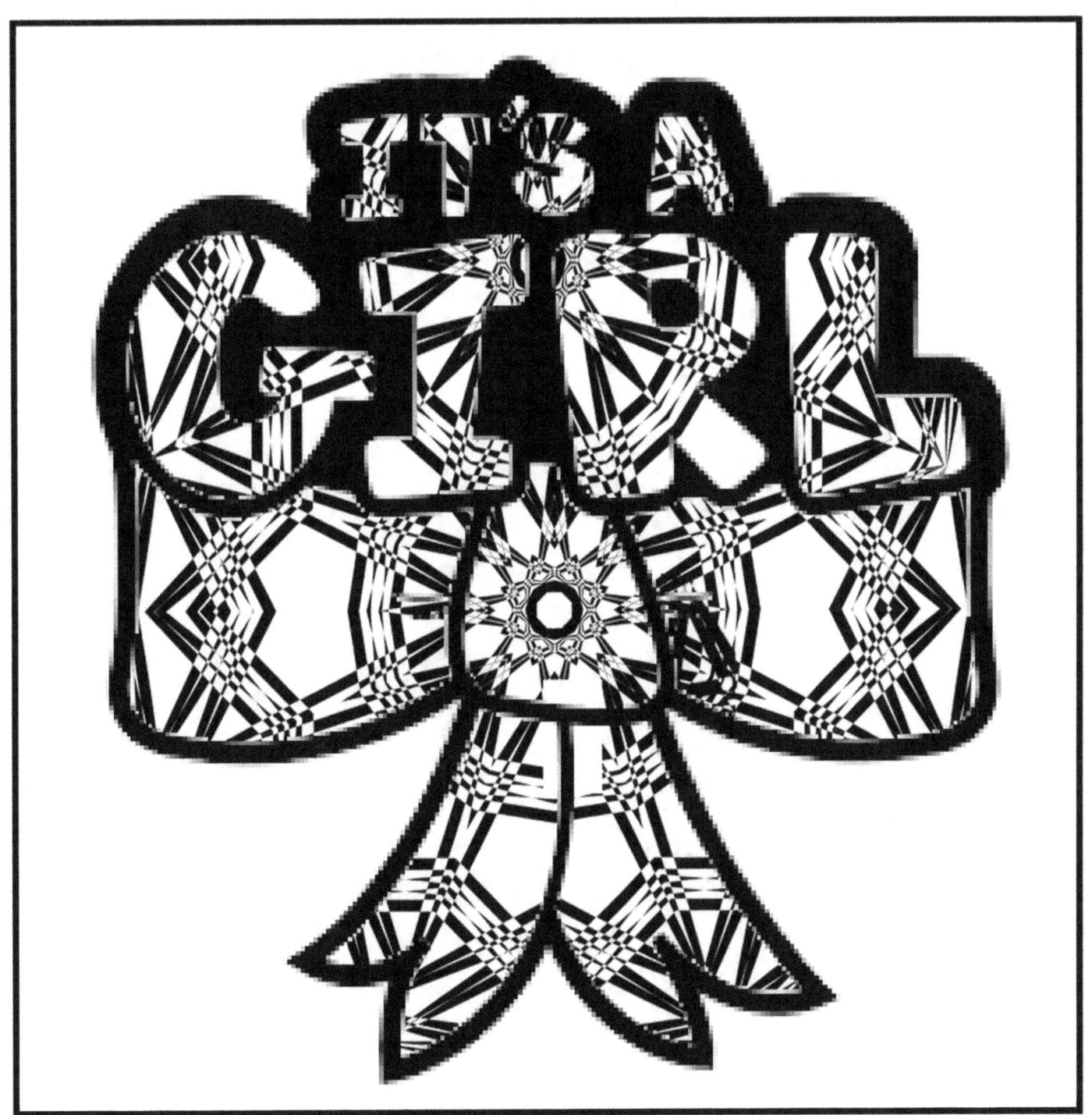

6. PREGNANT WOMAN SIDE PROFILE

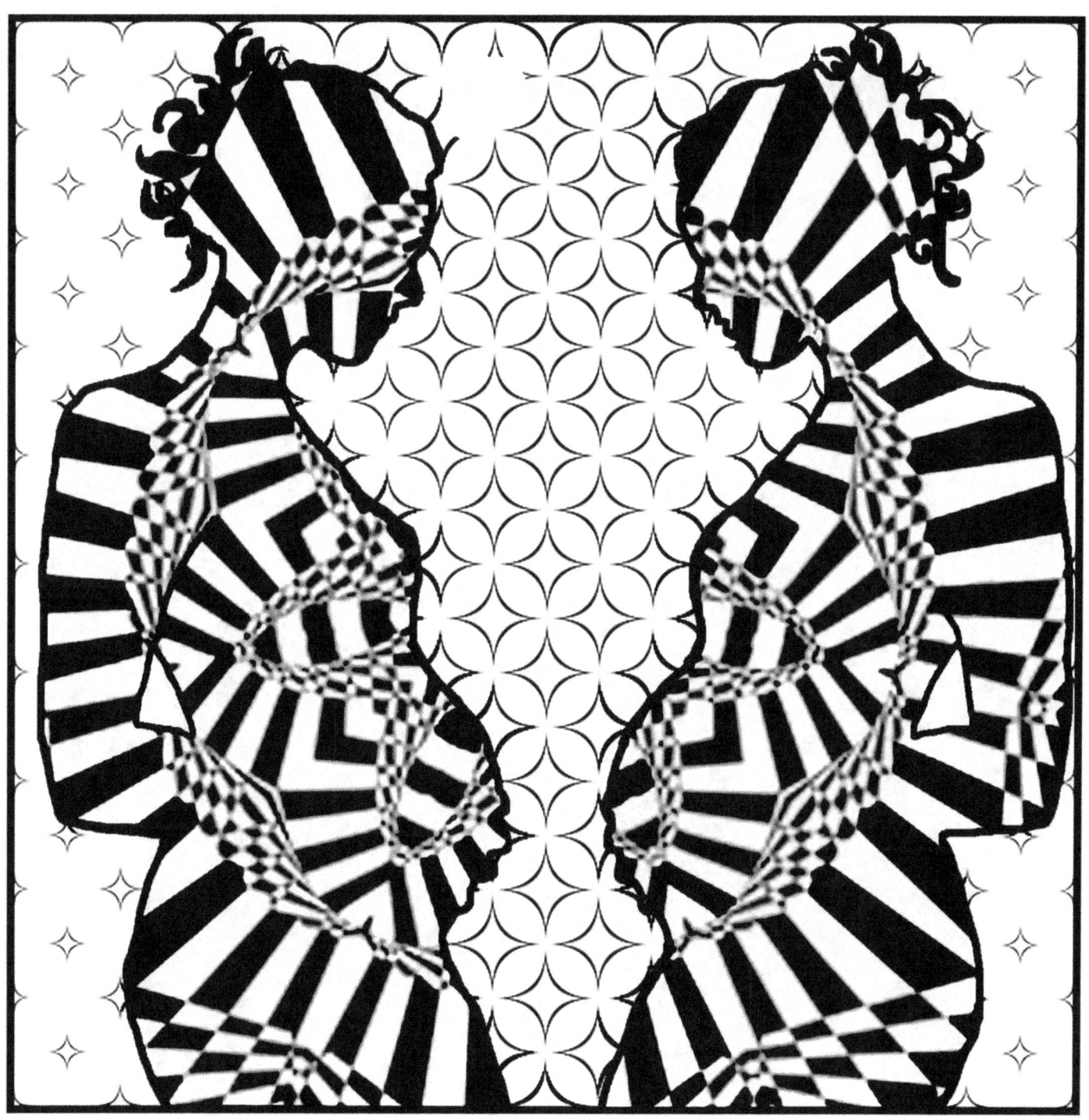

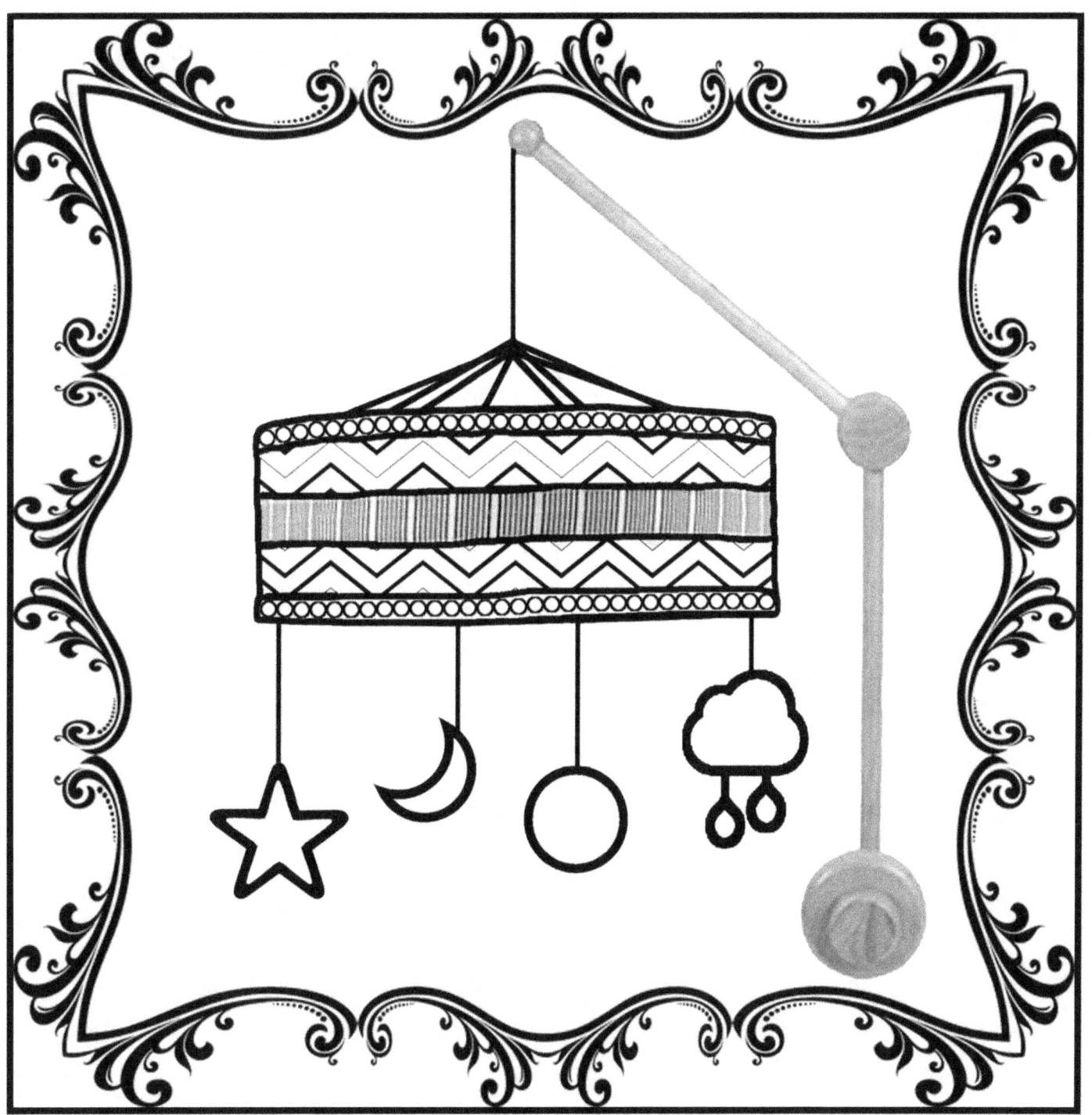

8. VINTAGE BABY CARRIAGE

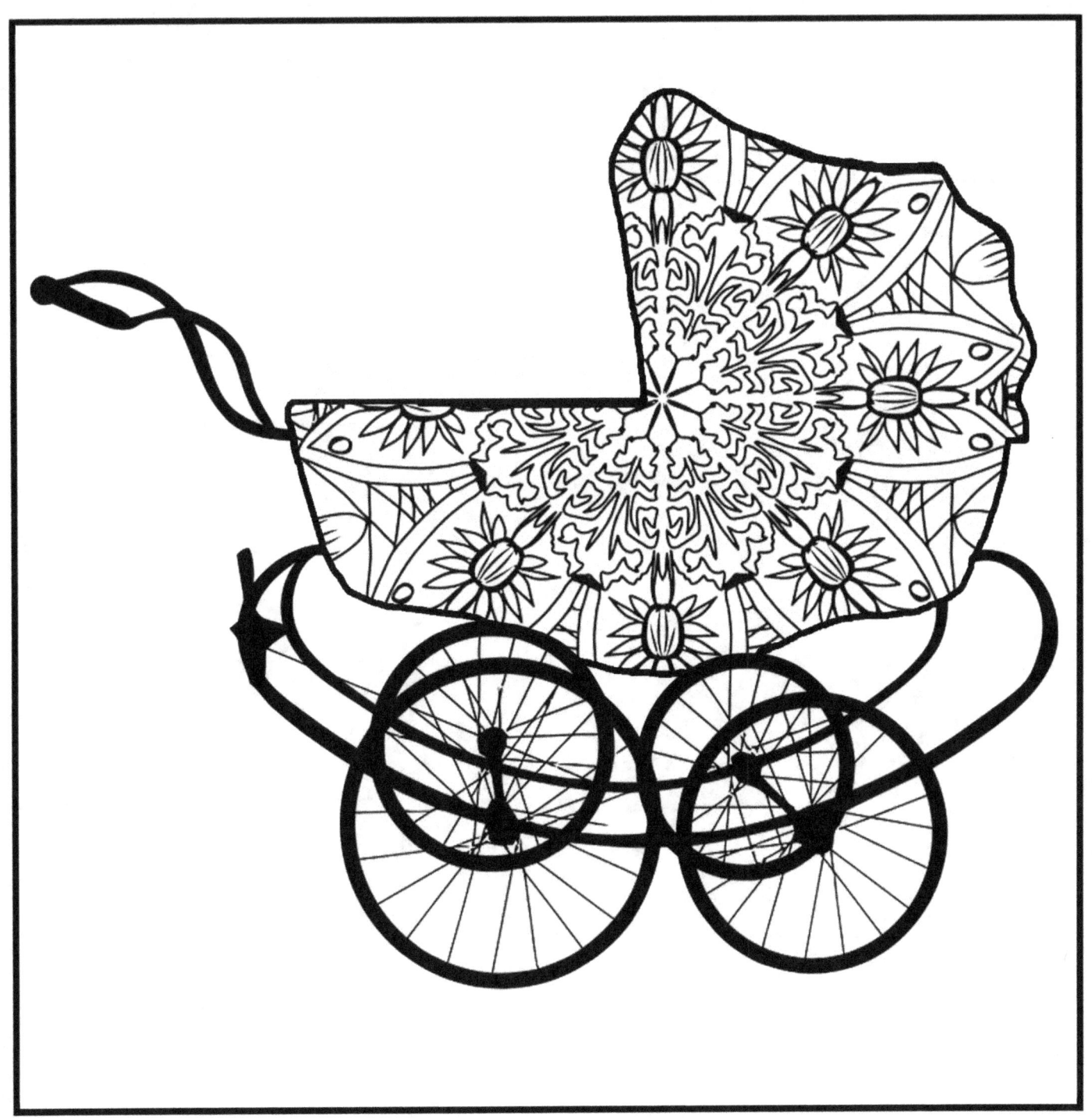

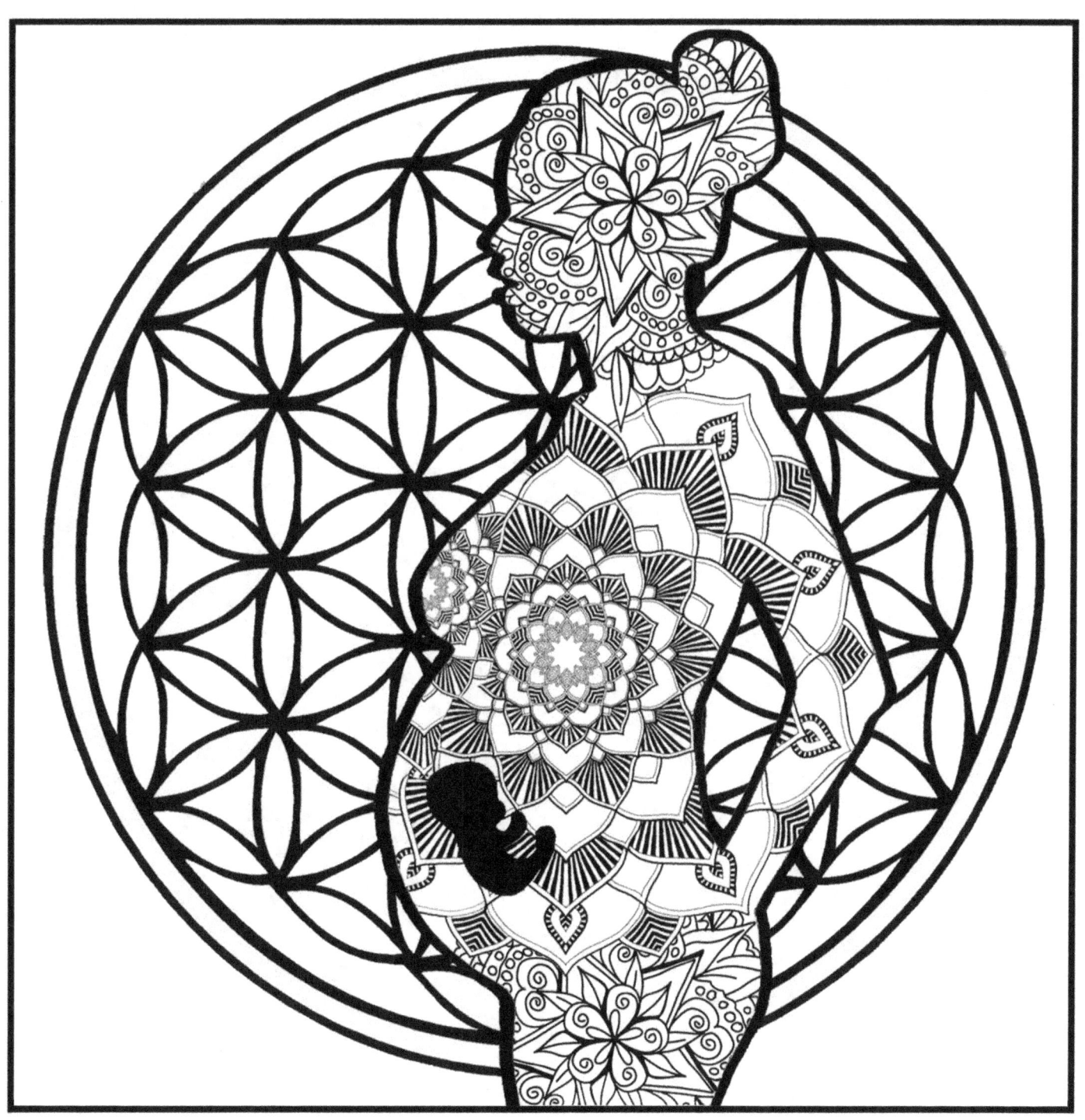

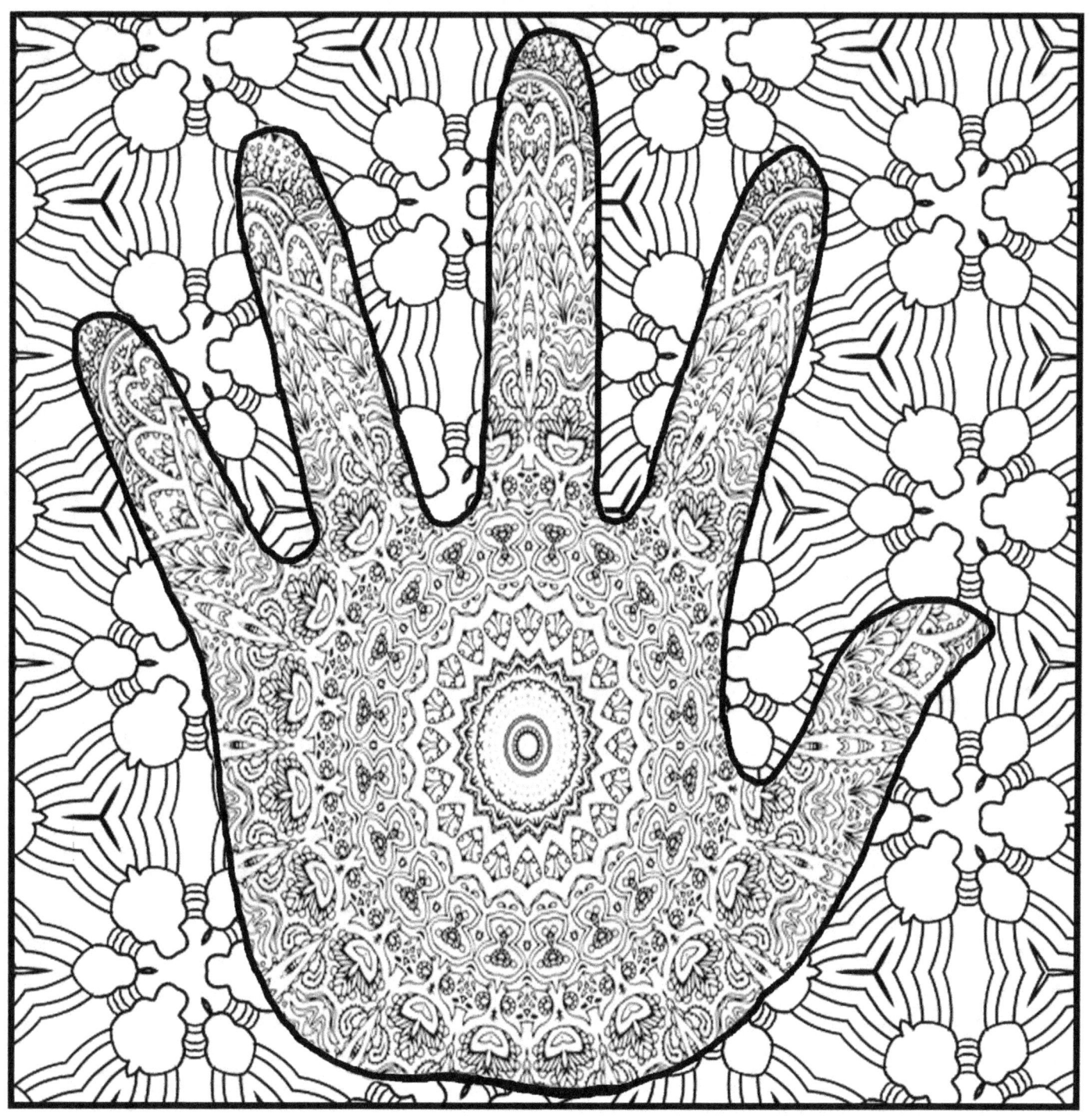

11. BABY CRIB

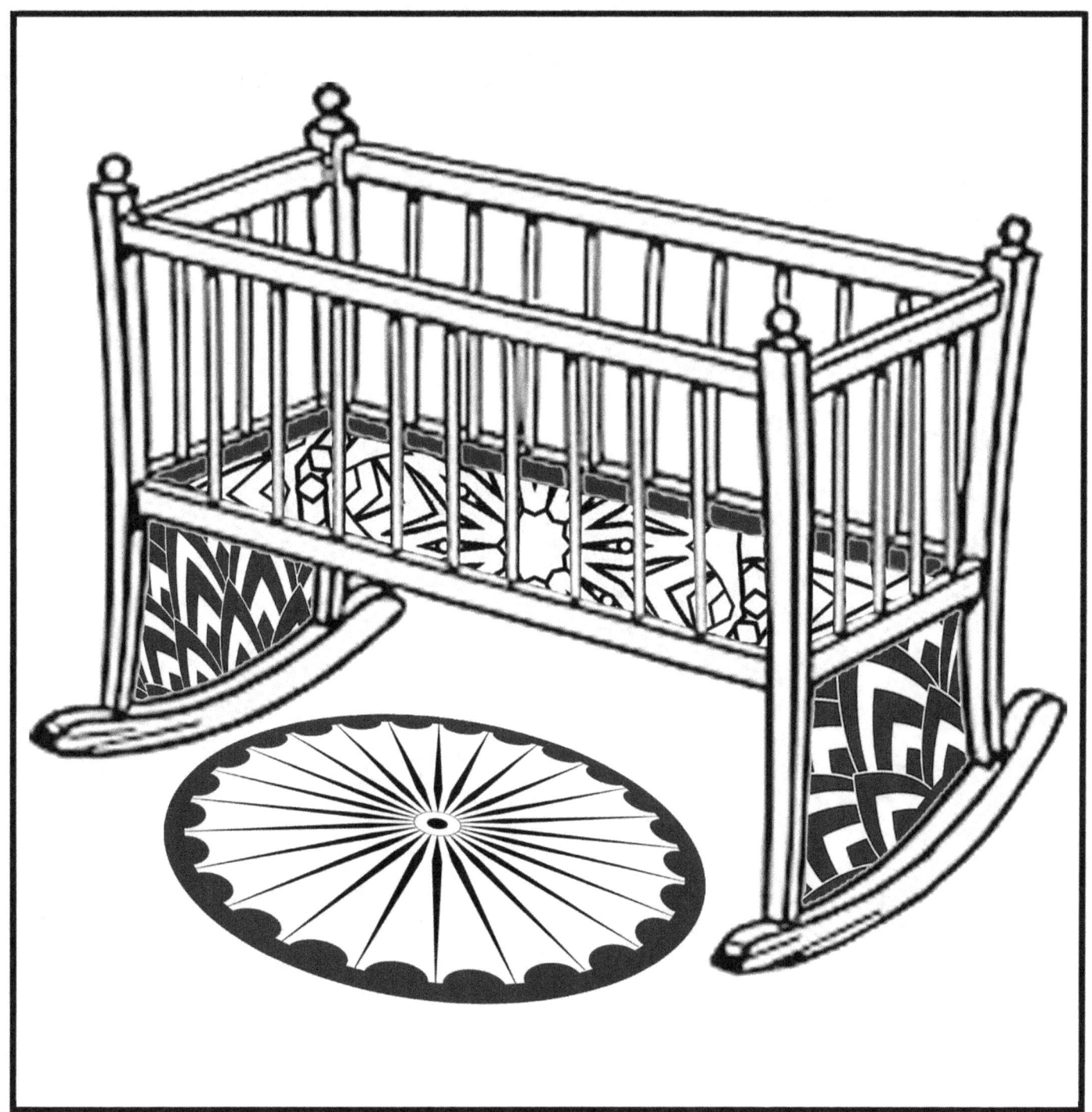

12. CLOTHES LINE

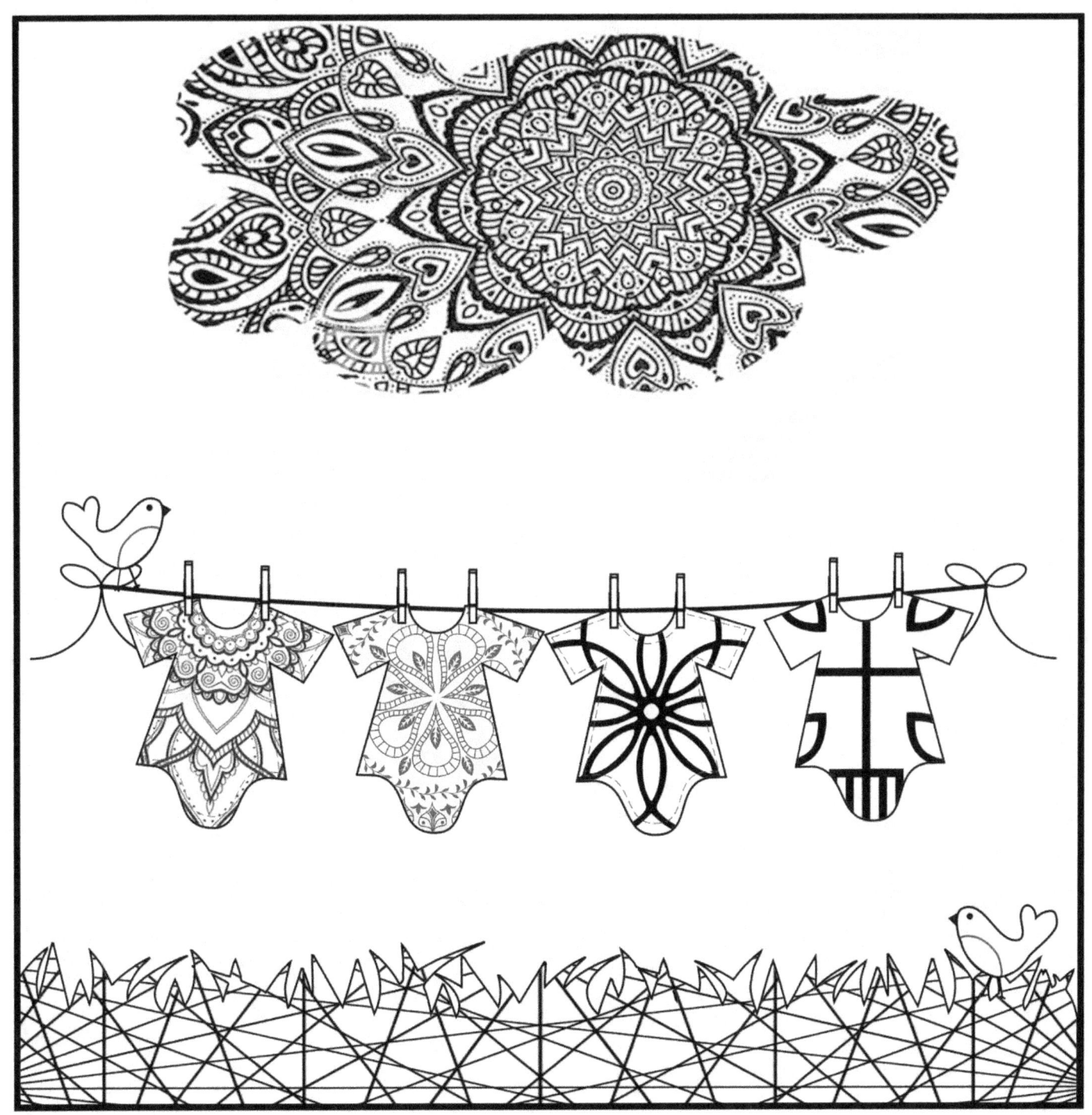

13. Baby Rattle

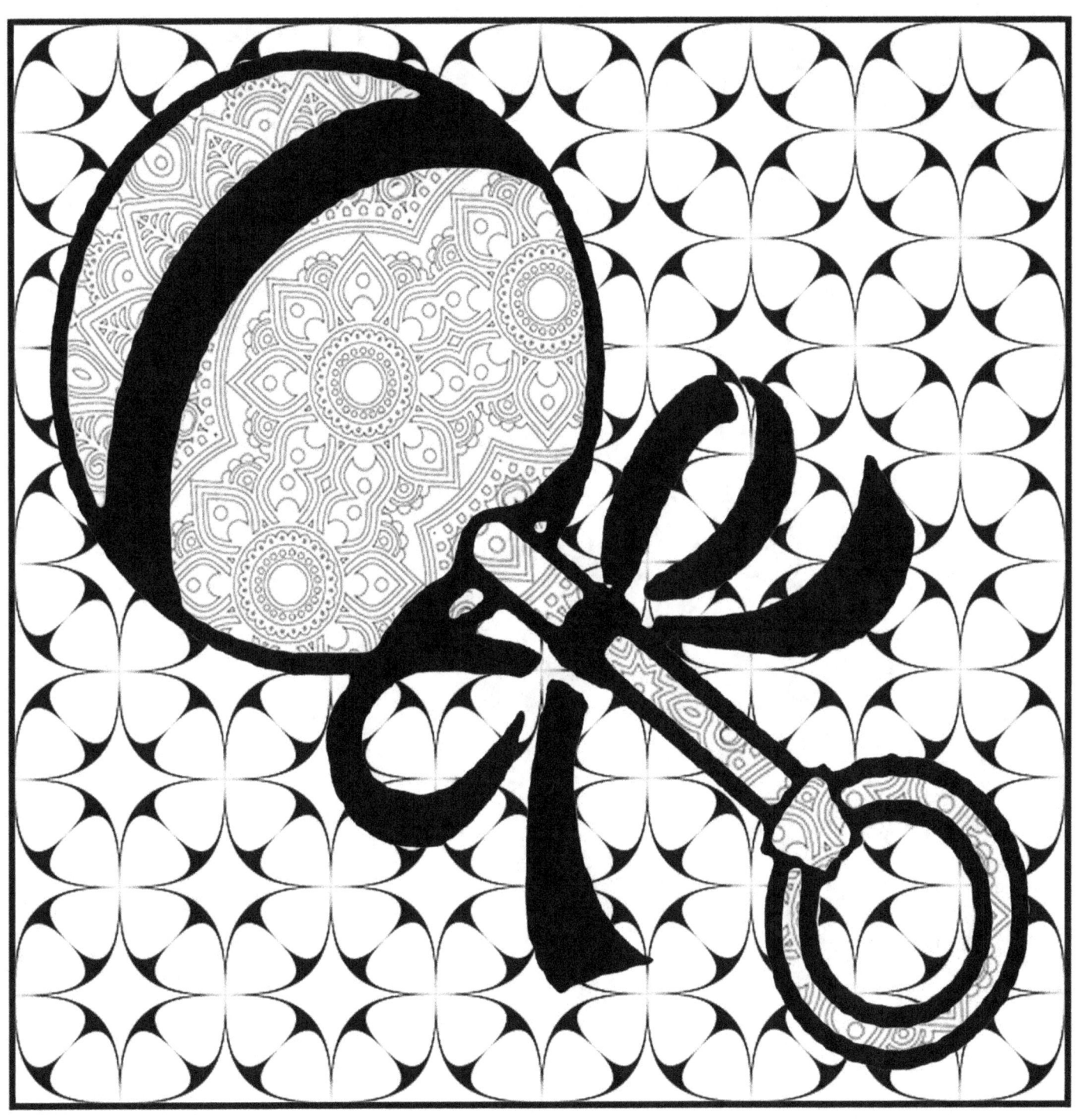

14. EXPECTING FATHER KISSING TUMMY

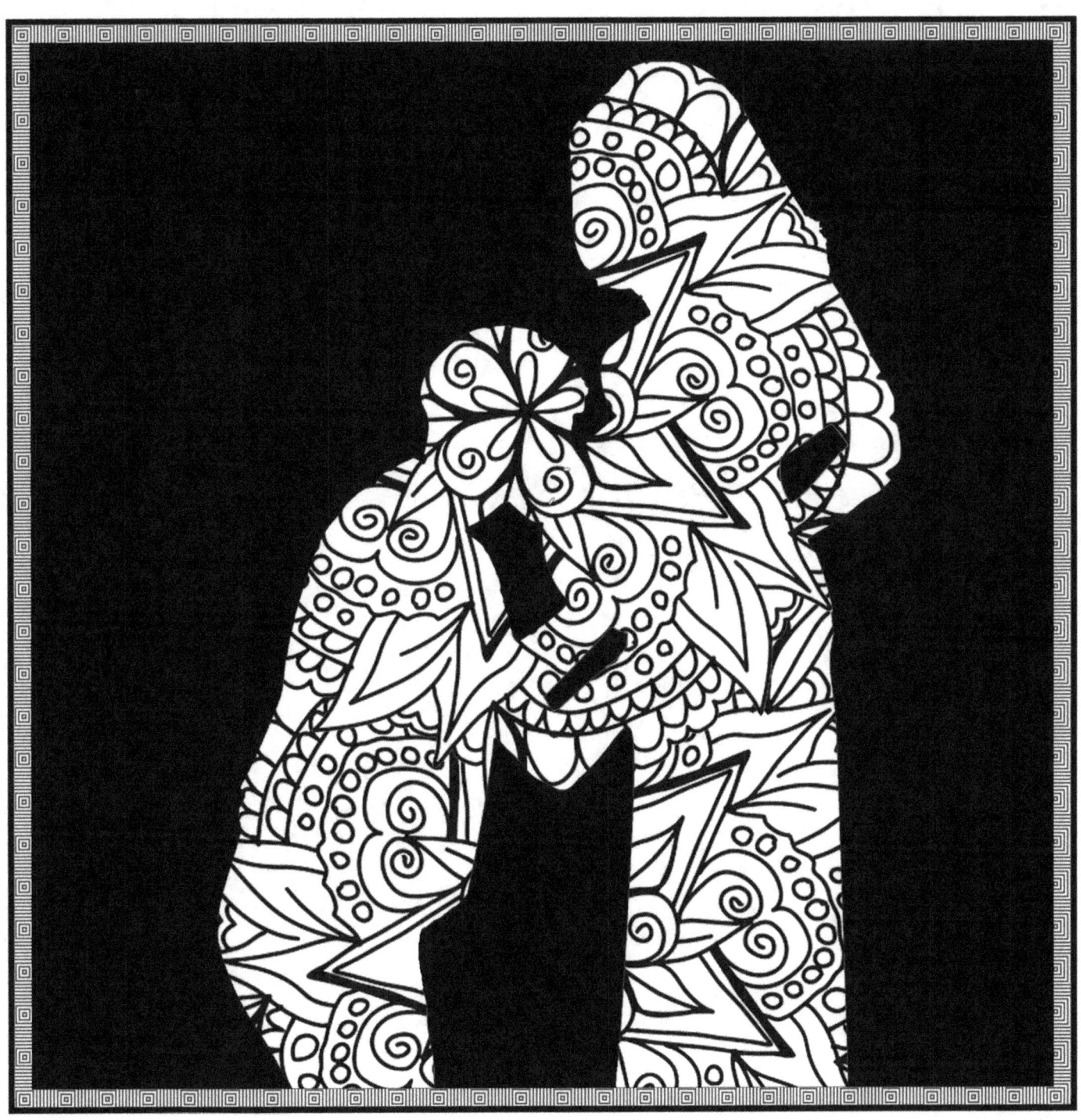

15. Vintage Baby Girl Dress

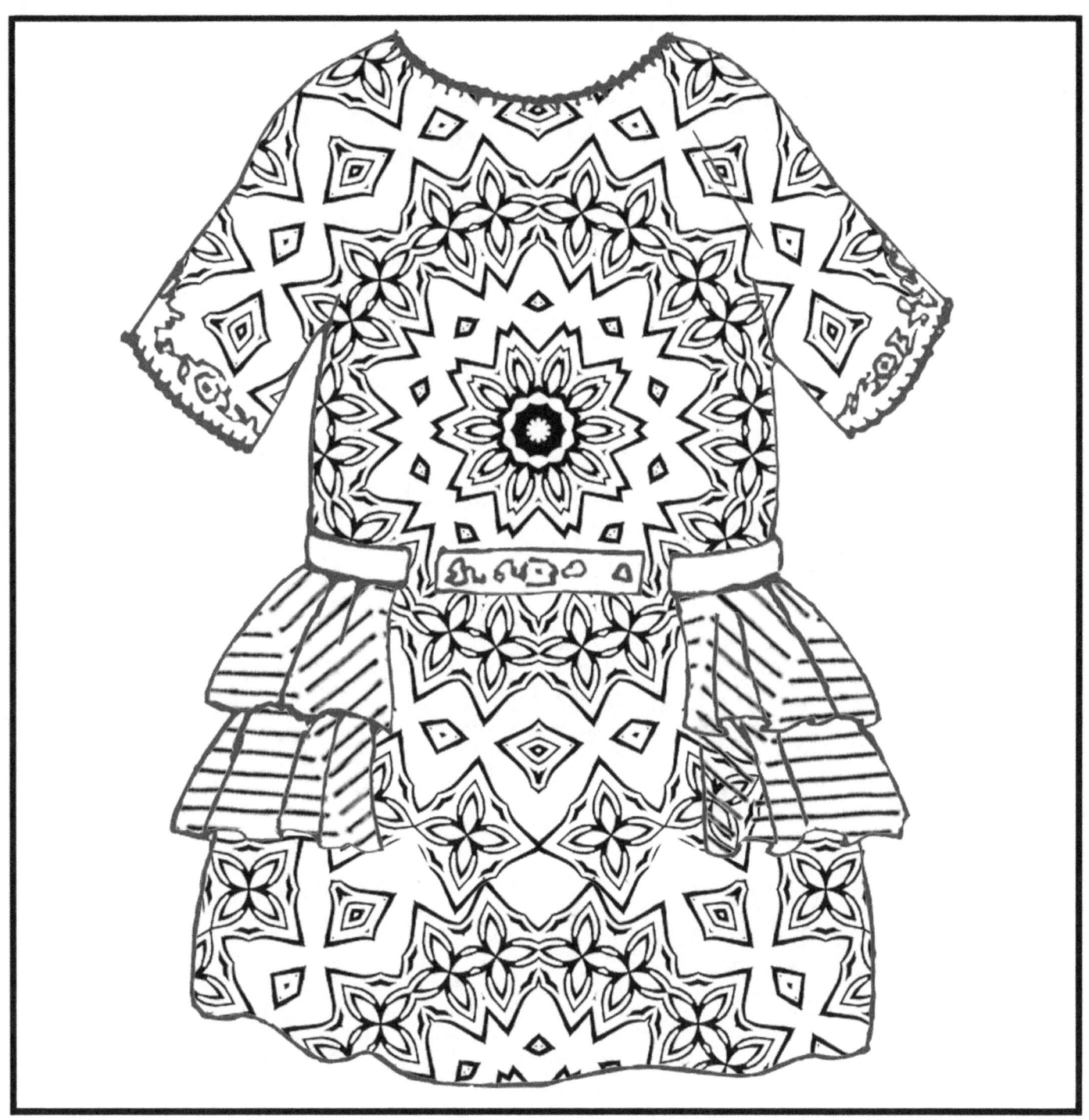

16. BABY SPOON

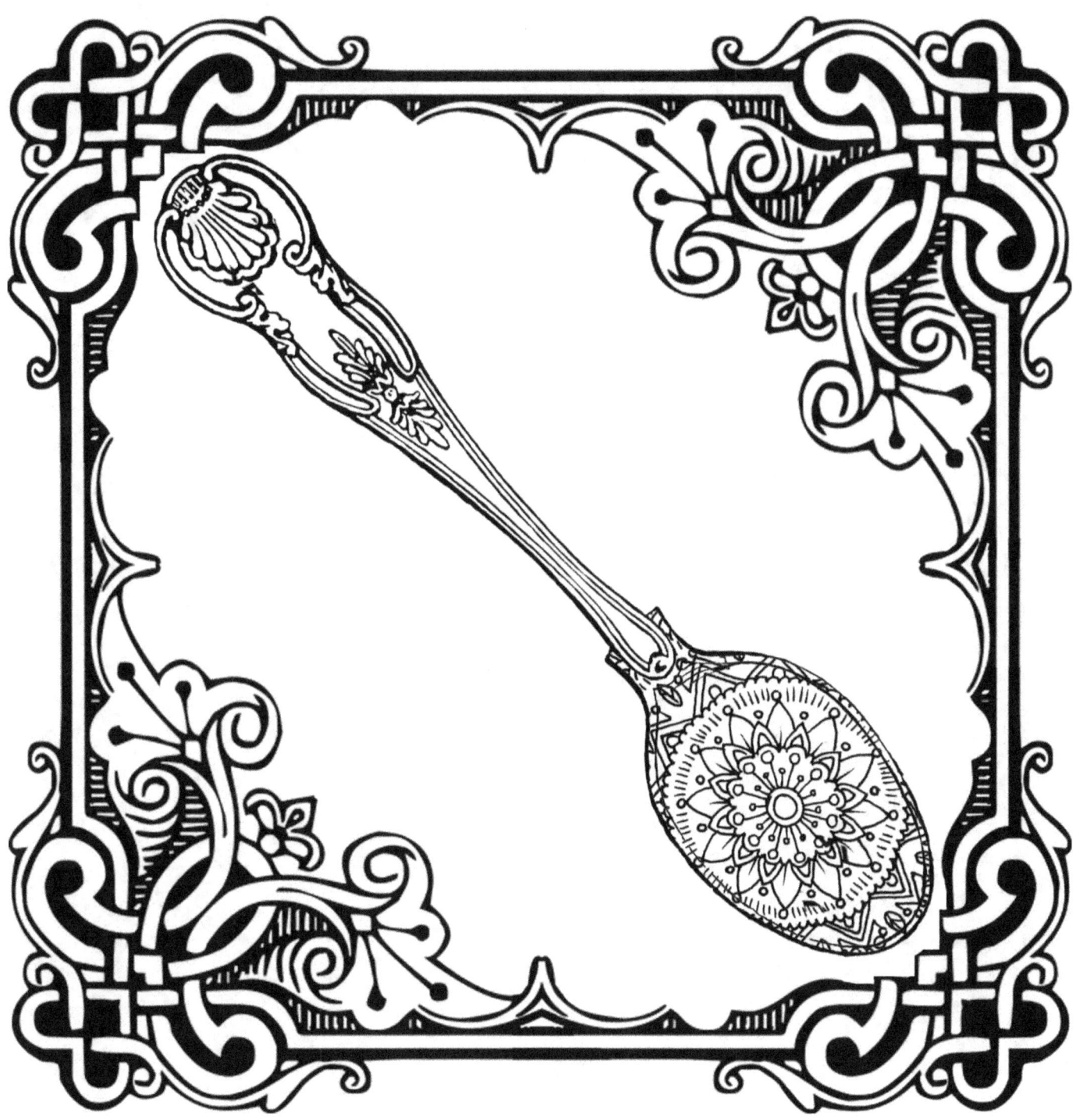

17. BABY BOUNCER

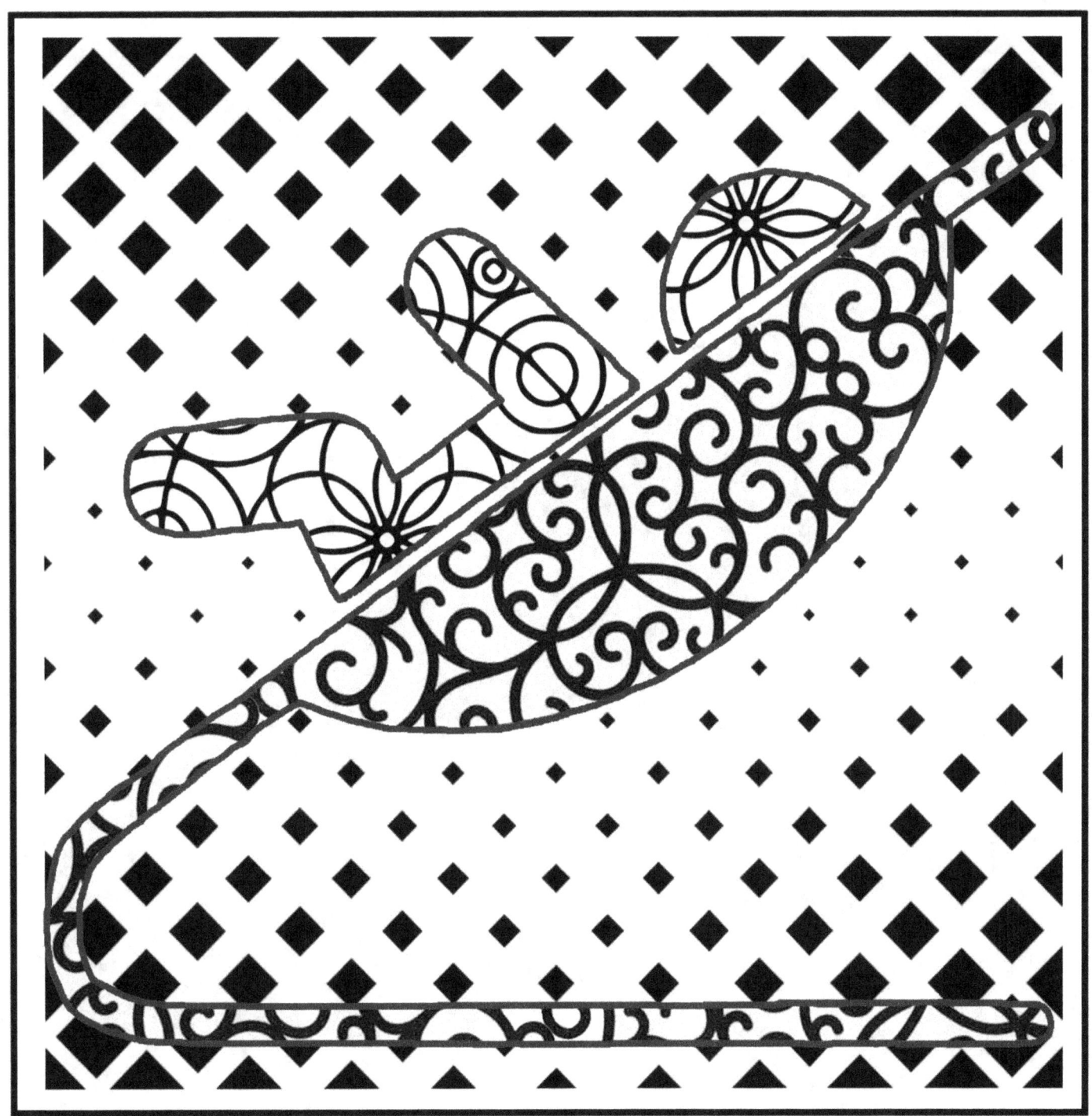

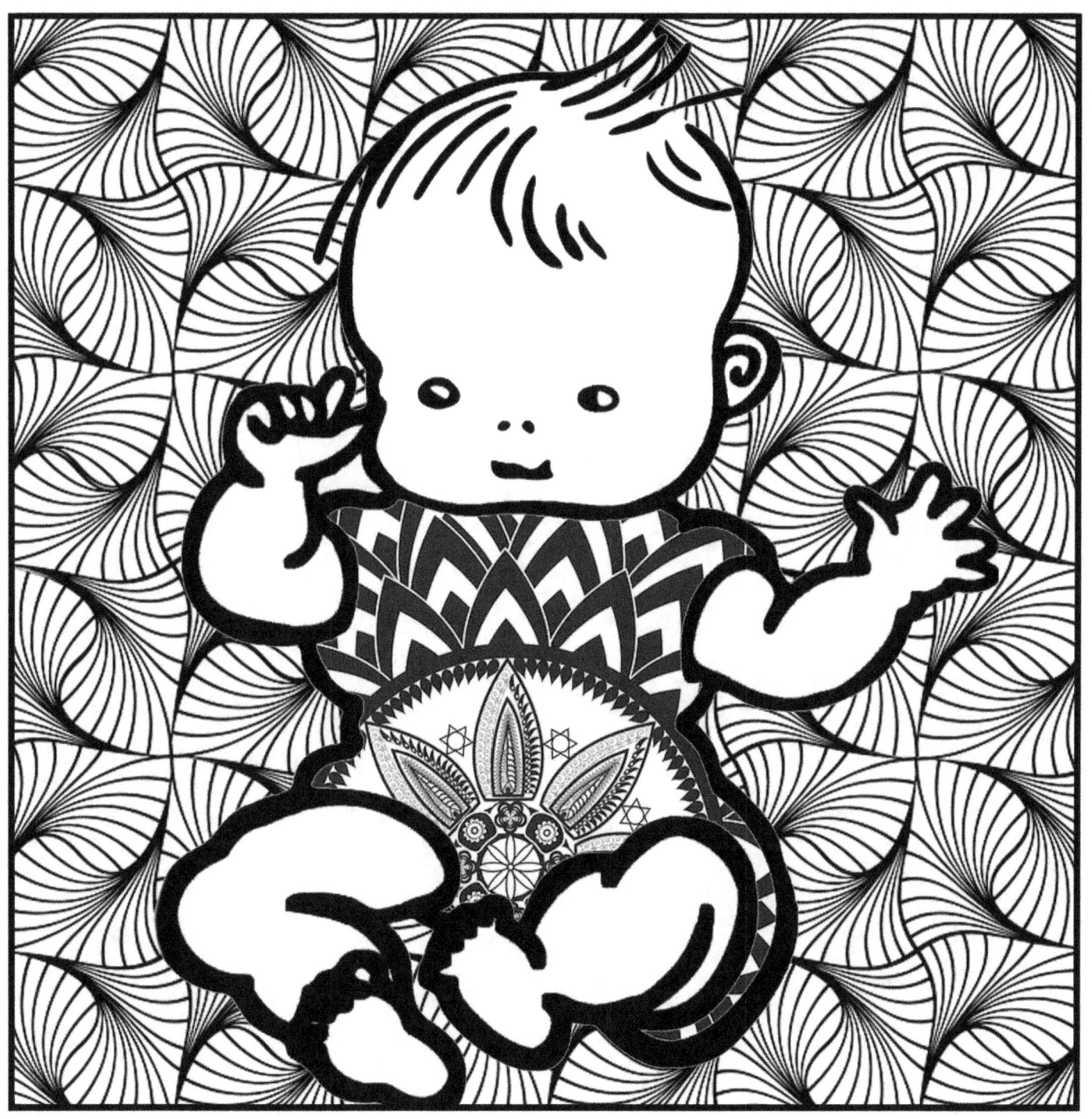

19. Breast Feeding

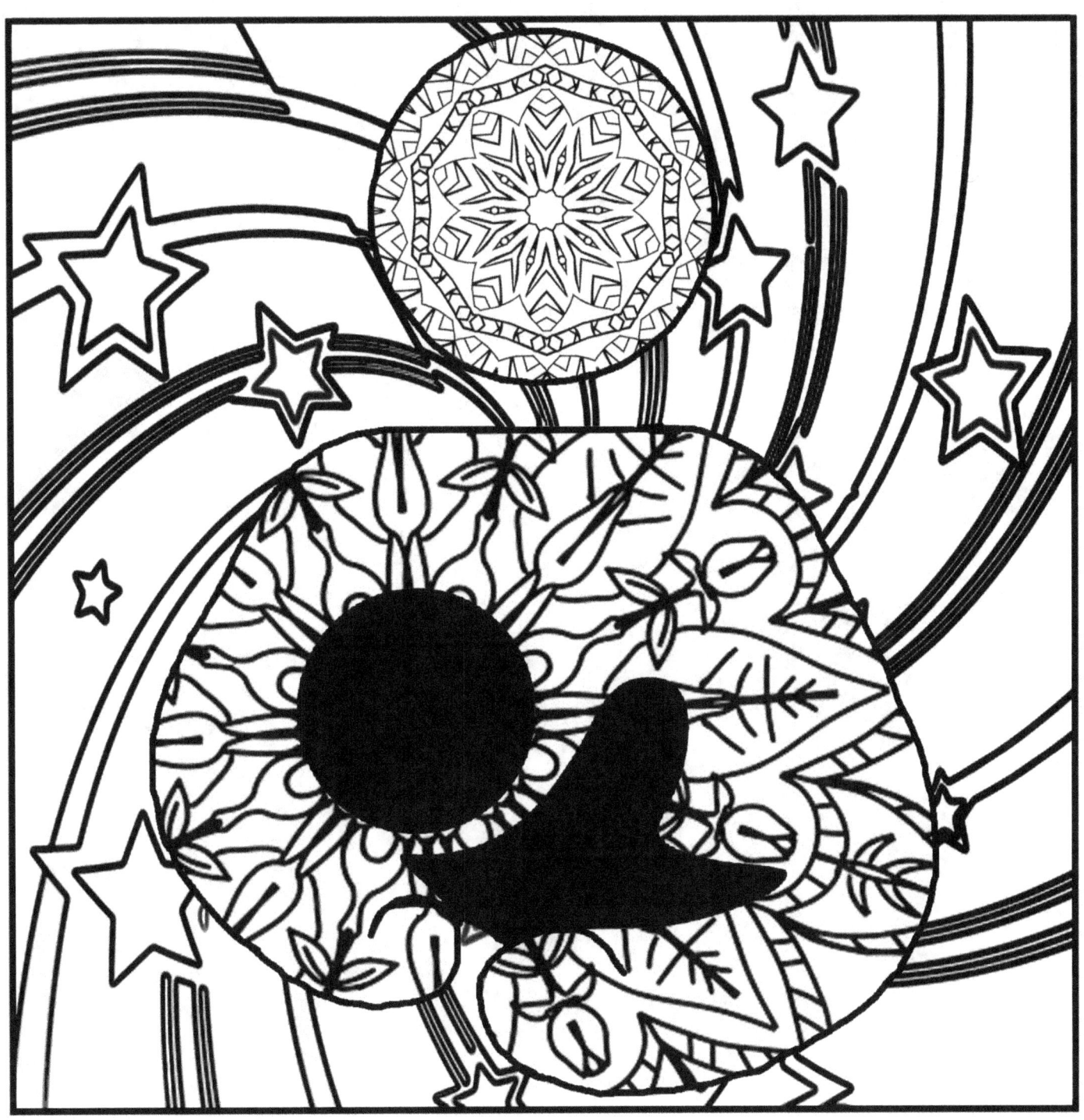

20. VINTAGE BIB

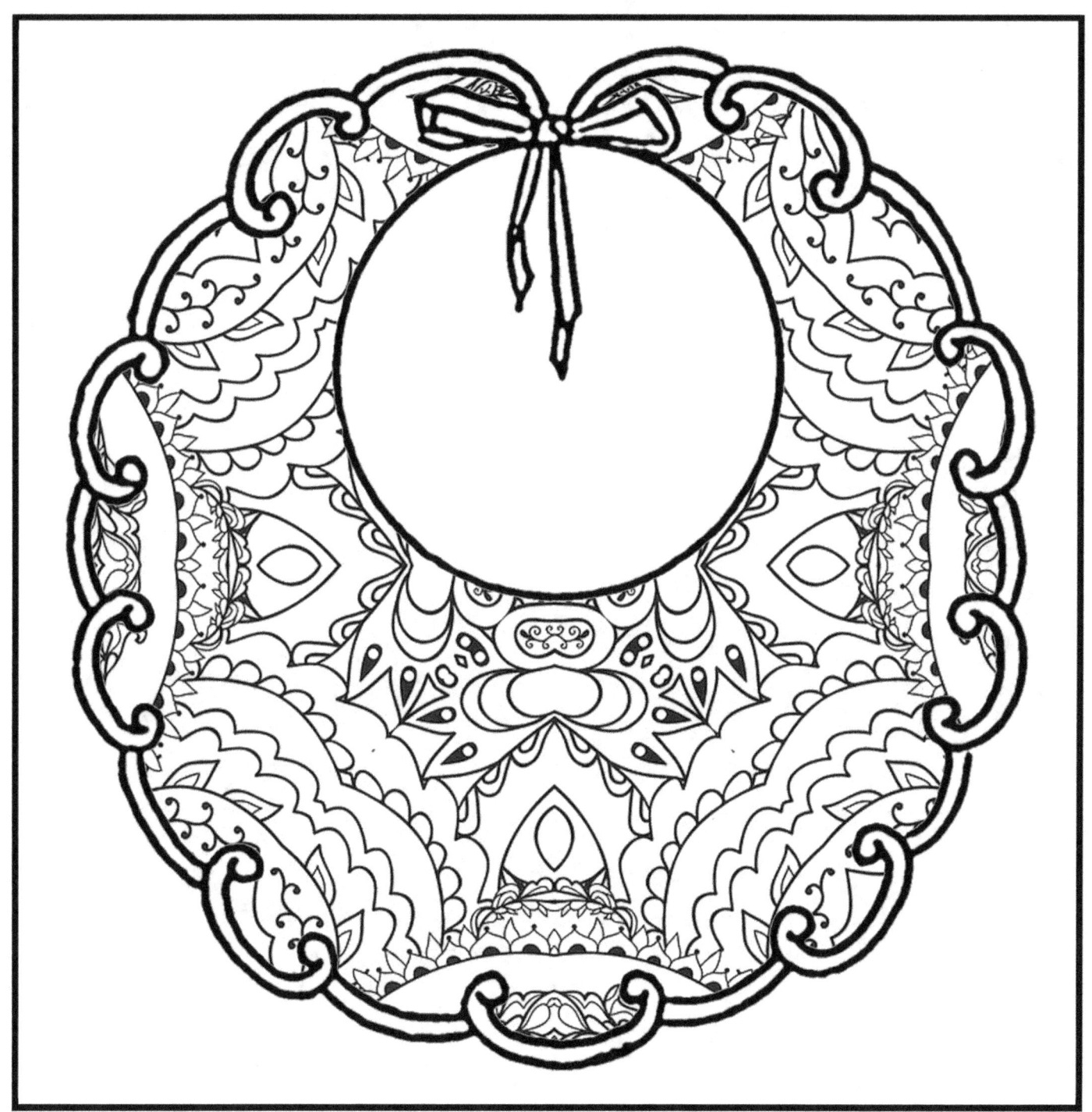

21. BABY BOY SPILLING MILK

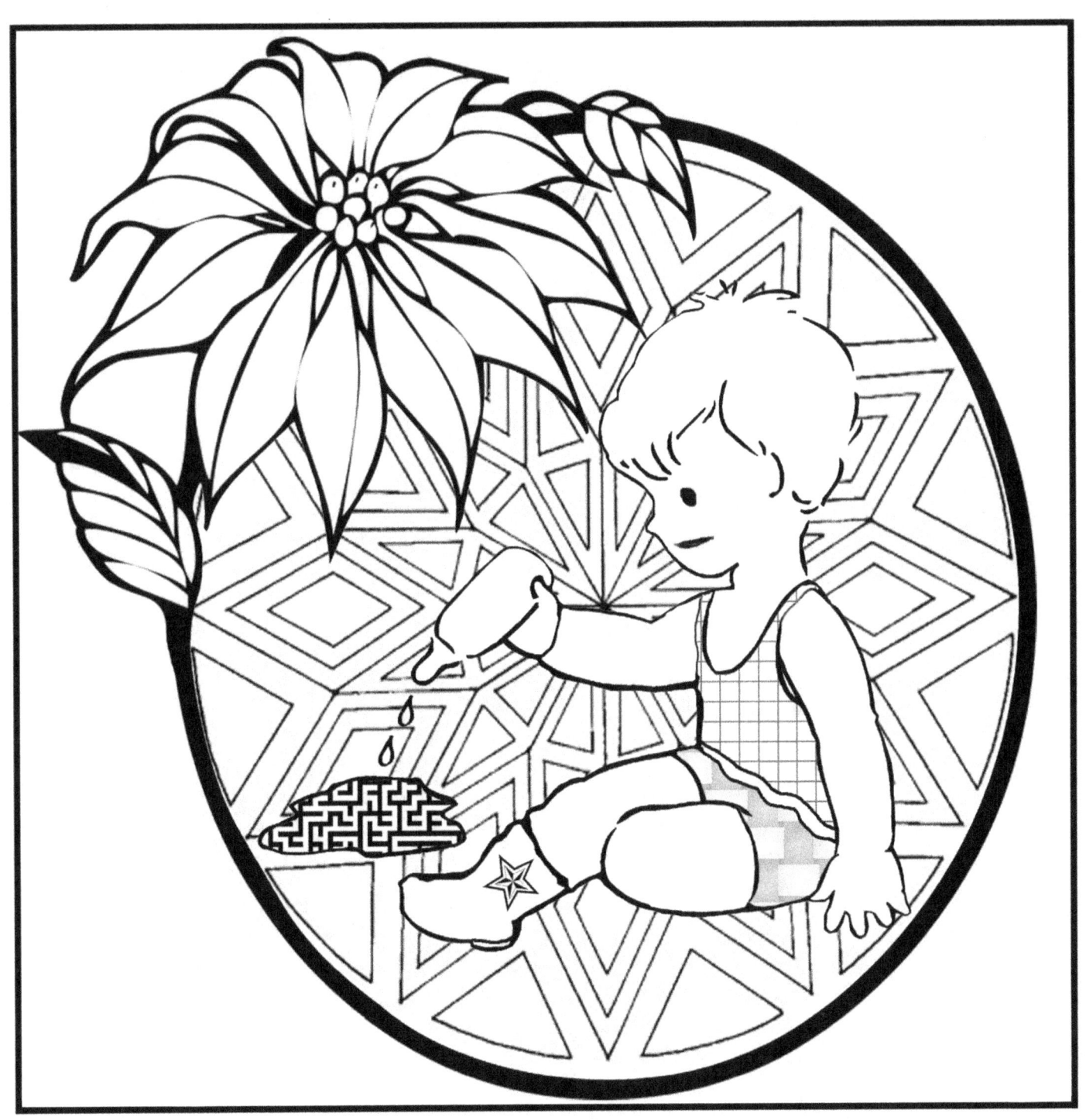

22. CLOTH DIAPER

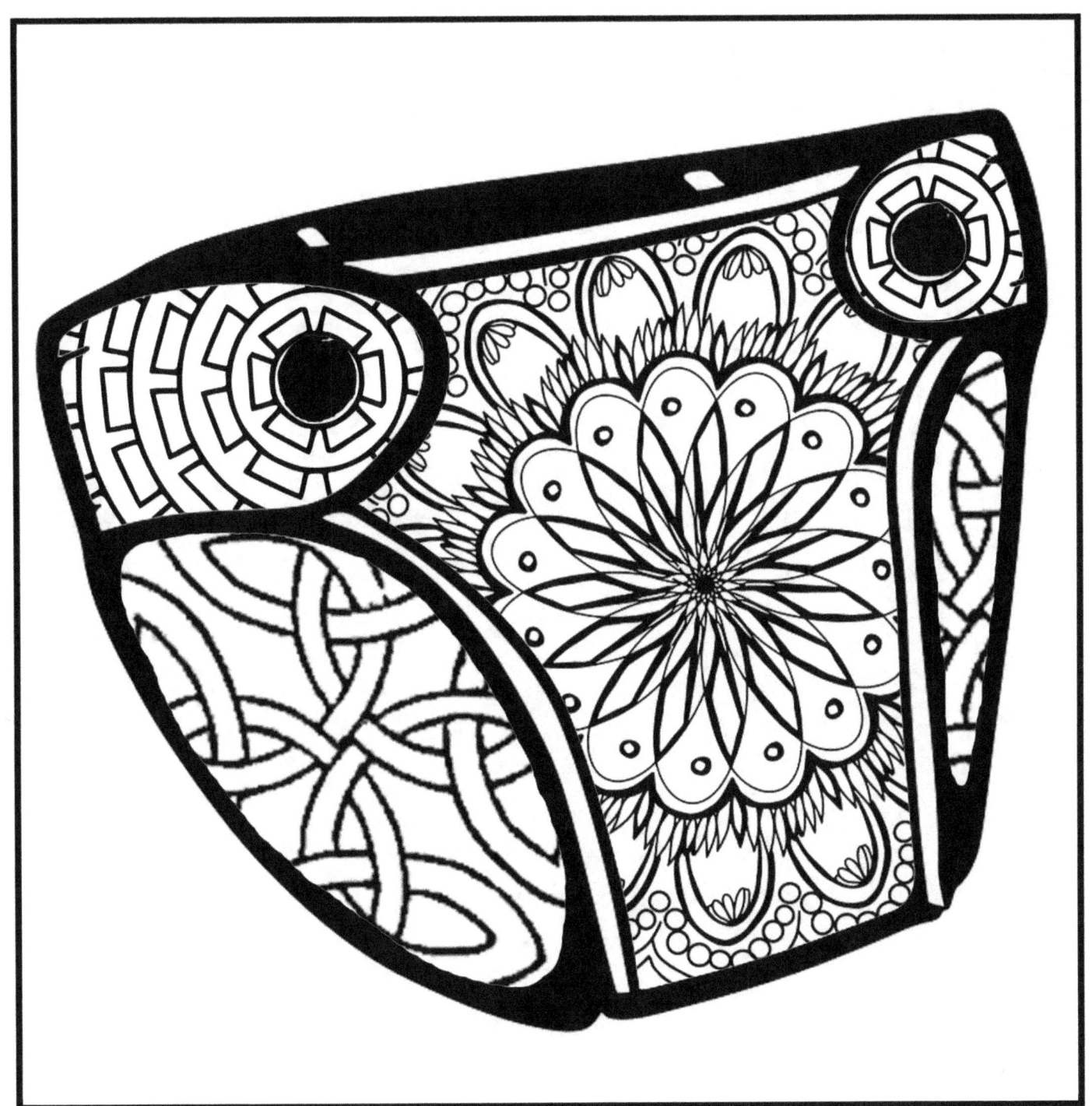

23. ROCKING HORSE

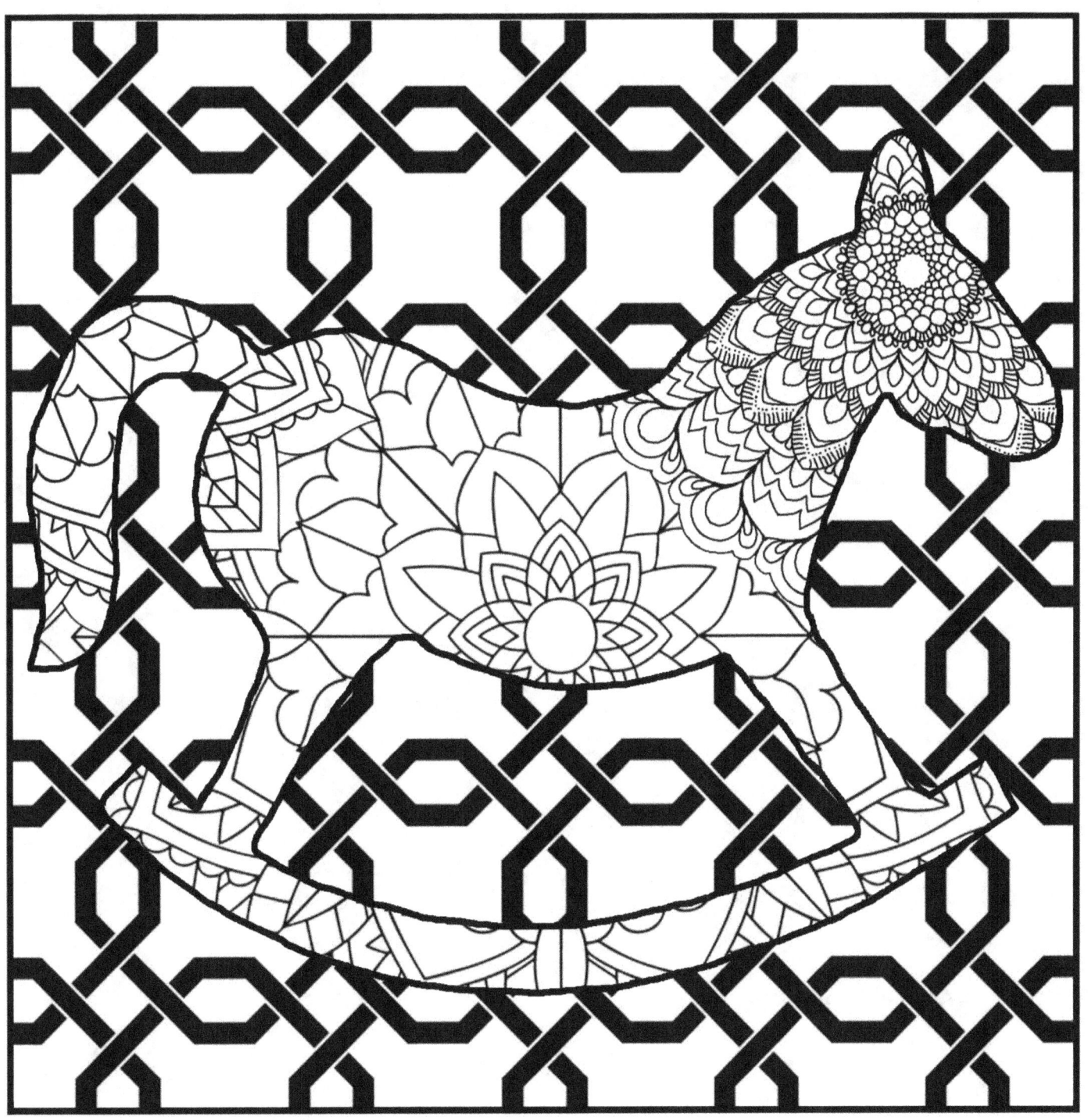

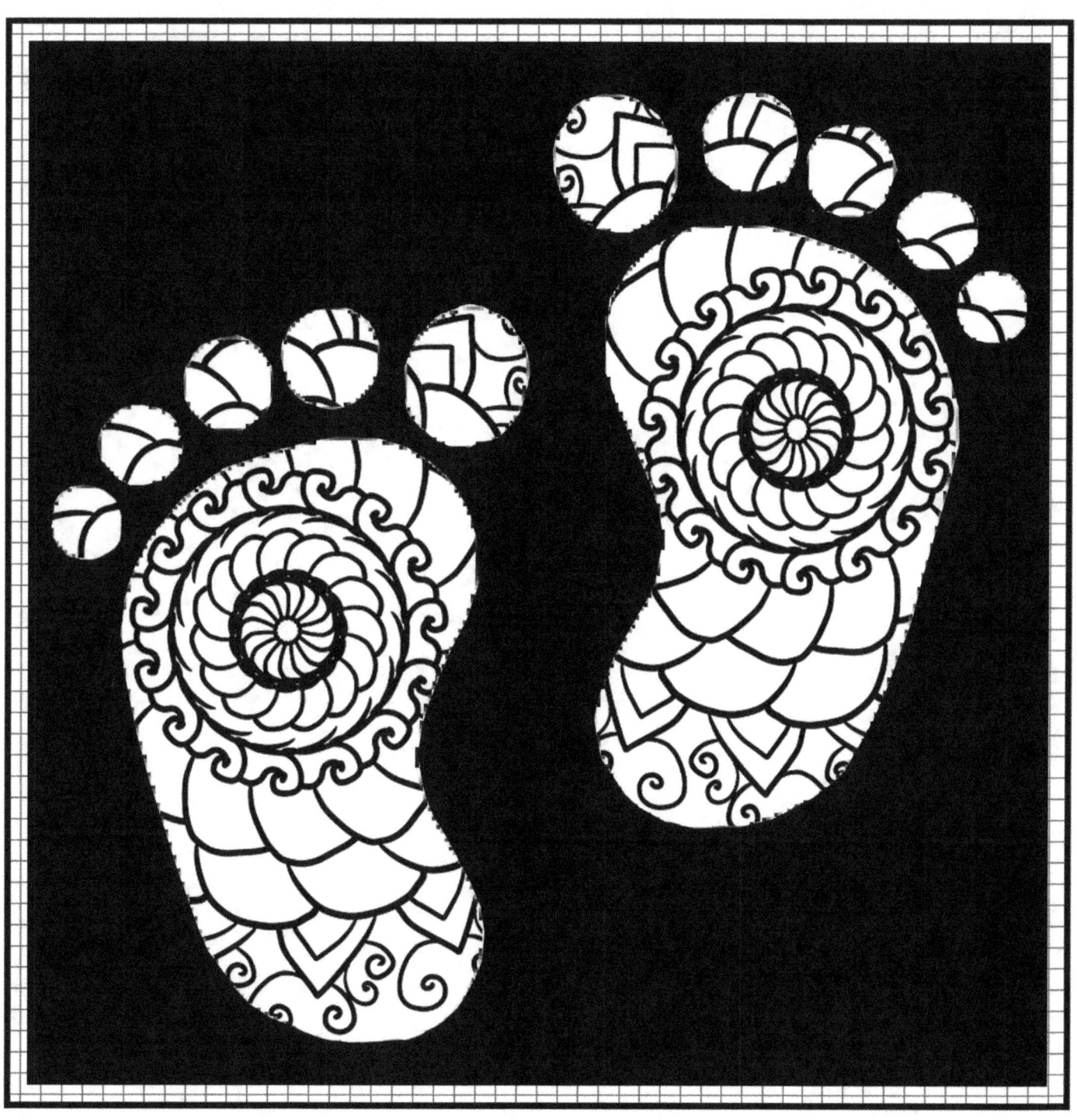

25. DAD WALKING WITH SON

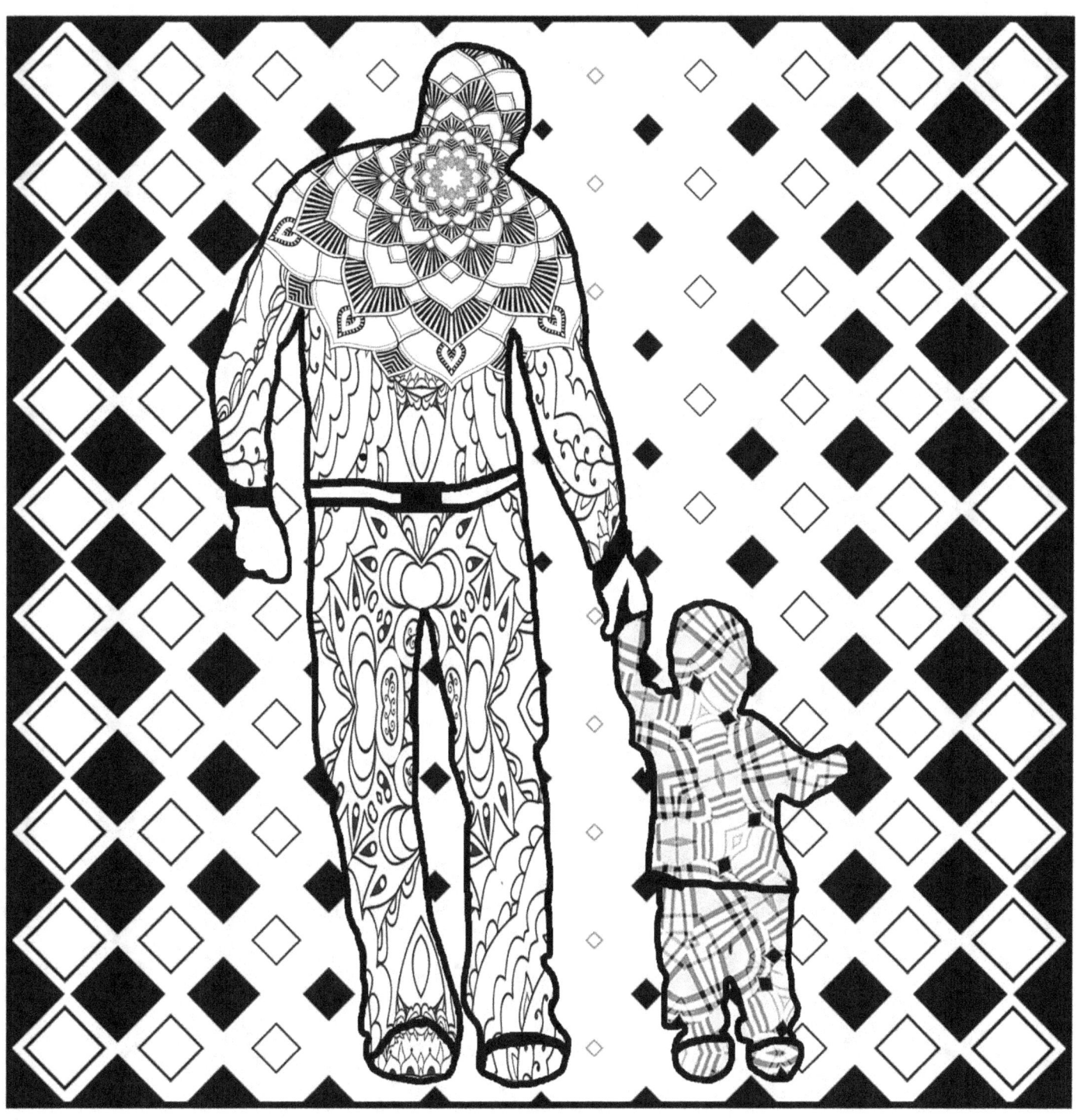

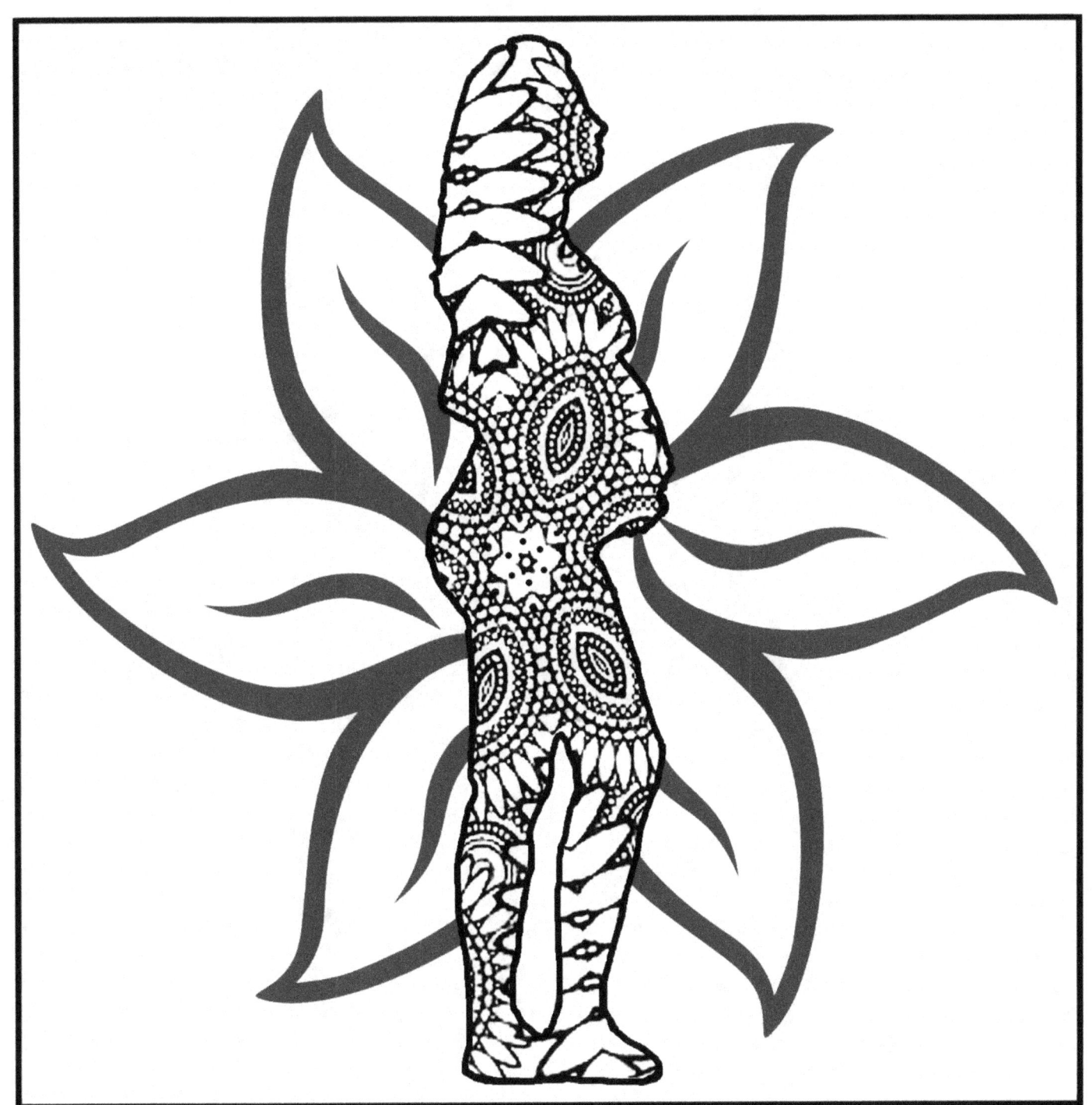

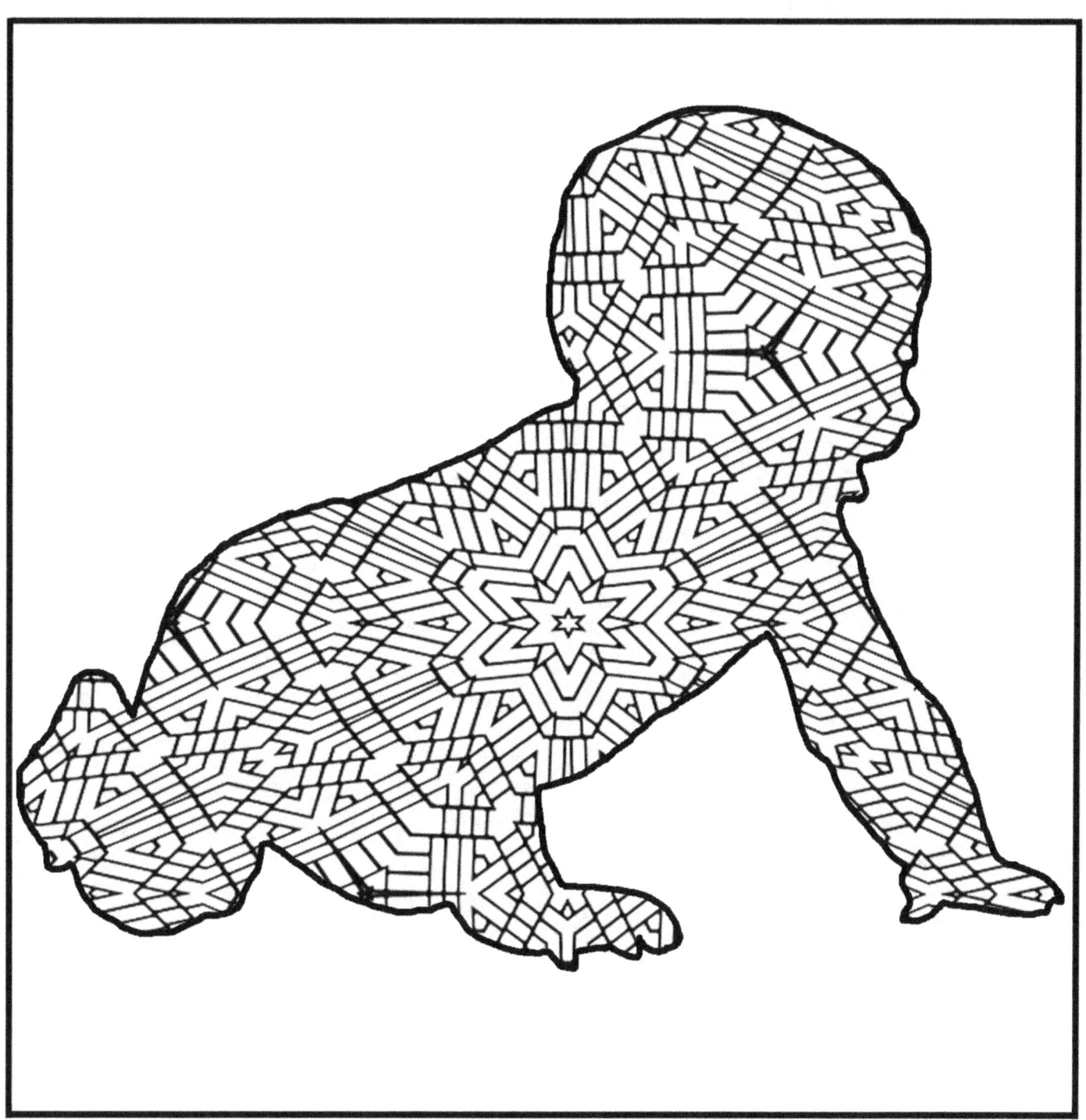

28. TEETHING RING

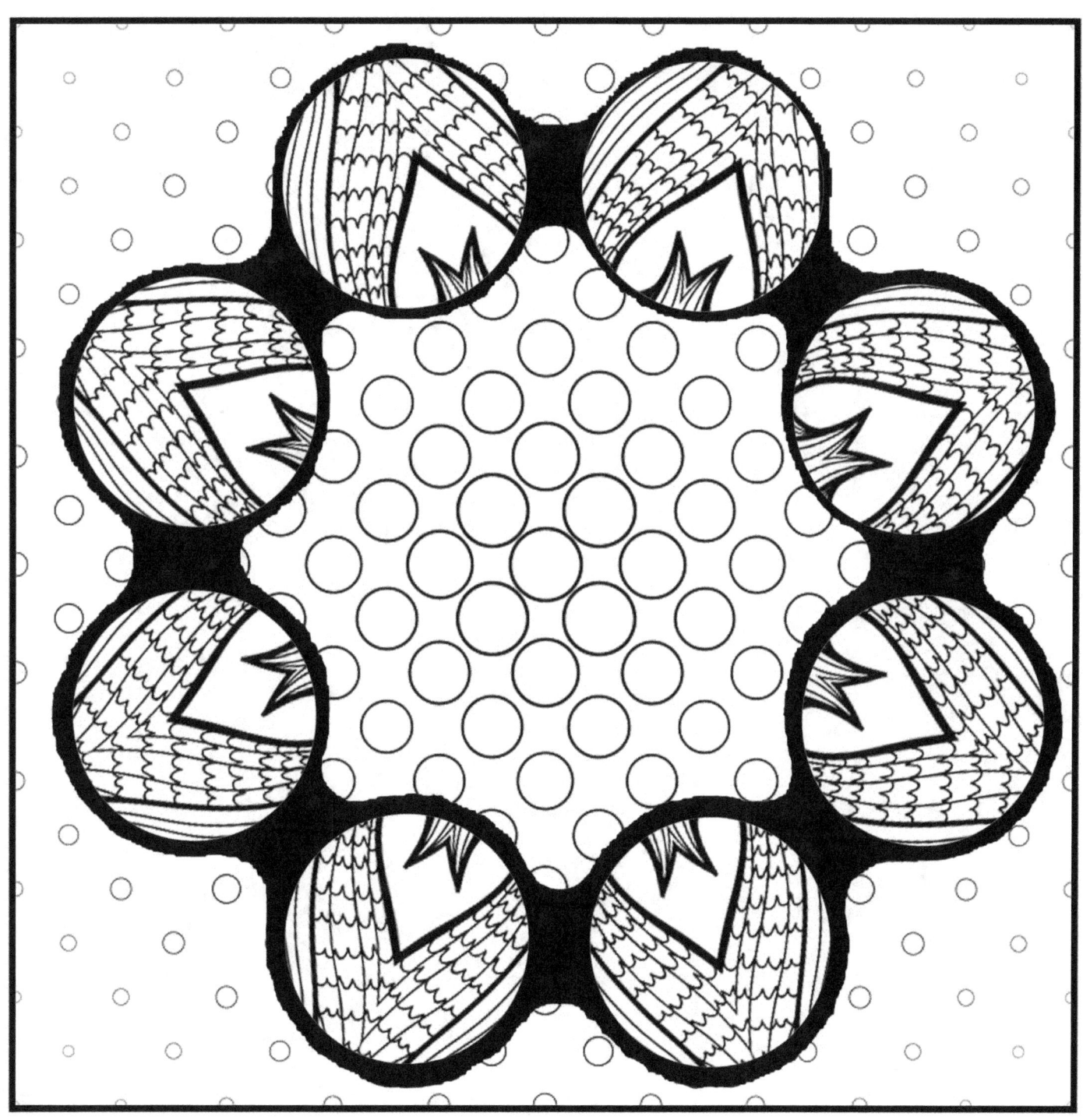

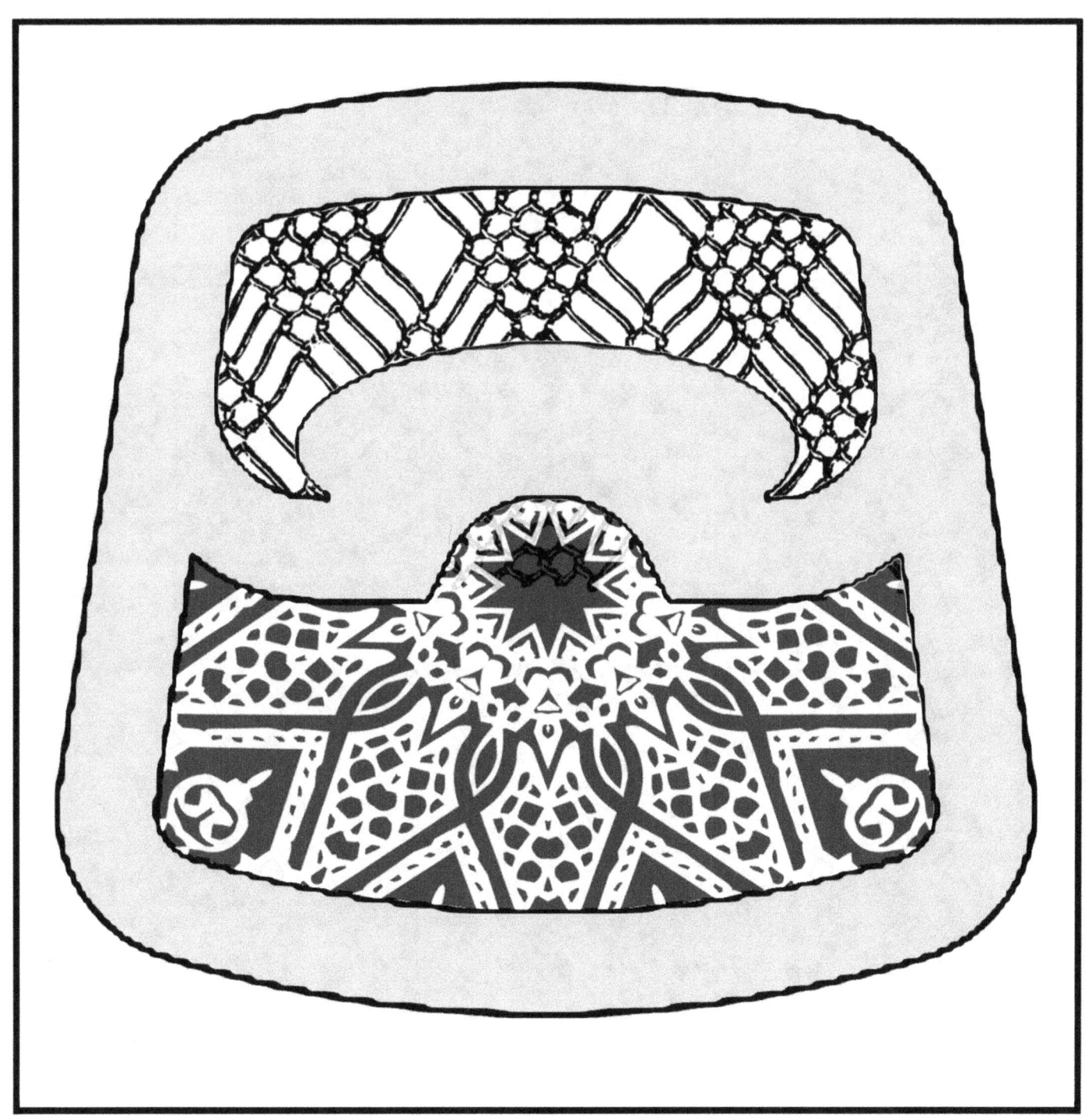

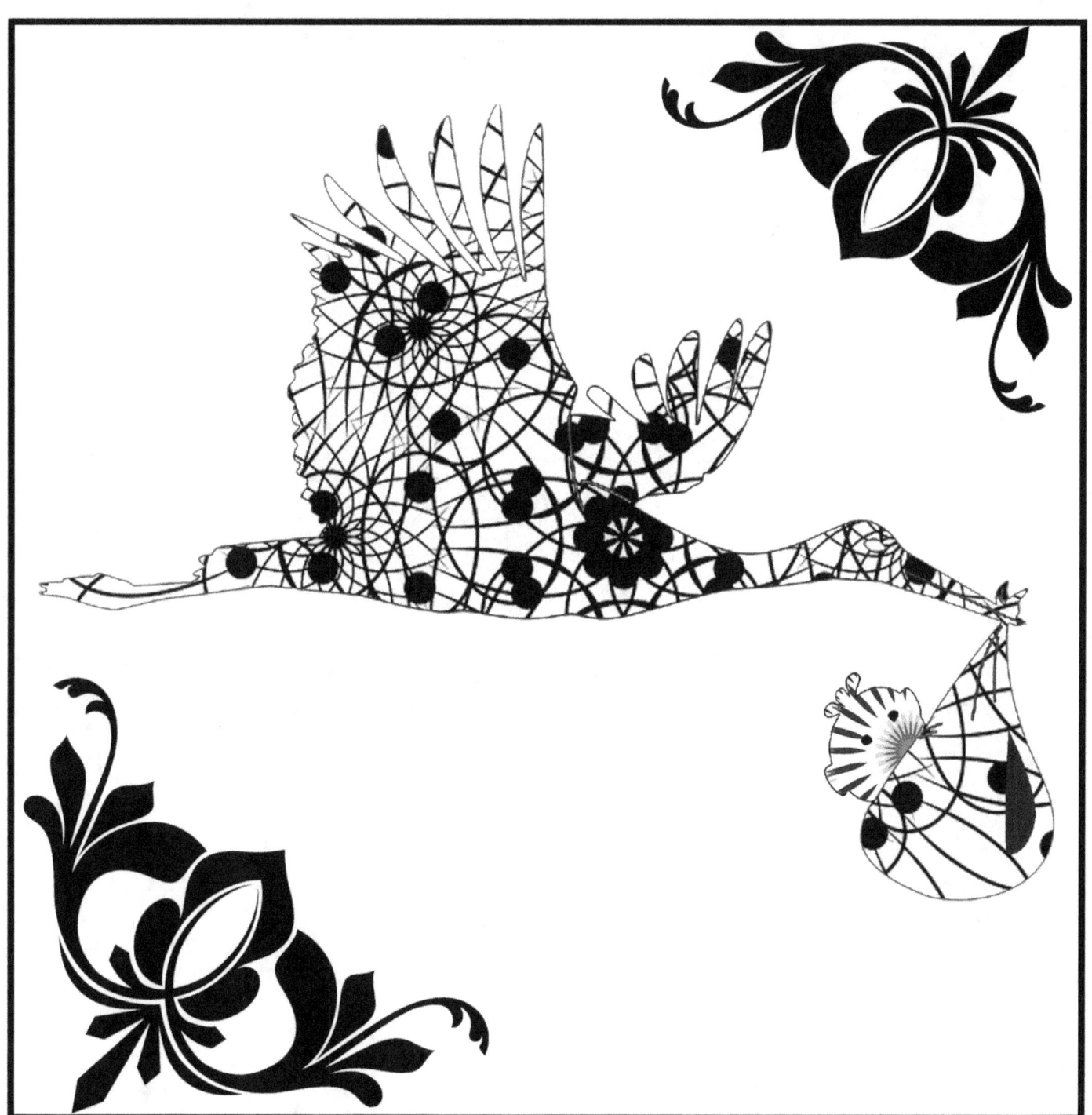

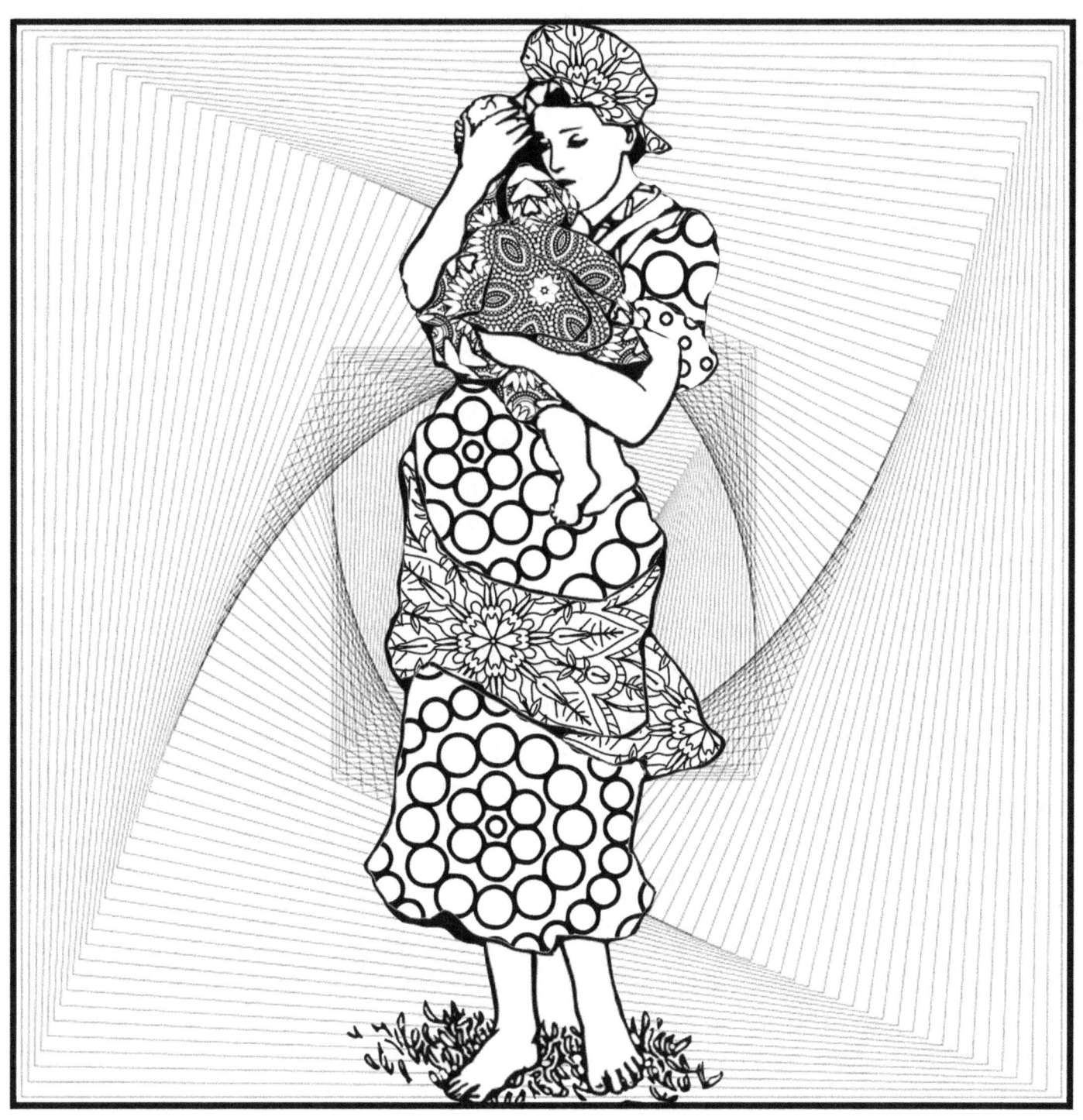

32. LAYING BABY

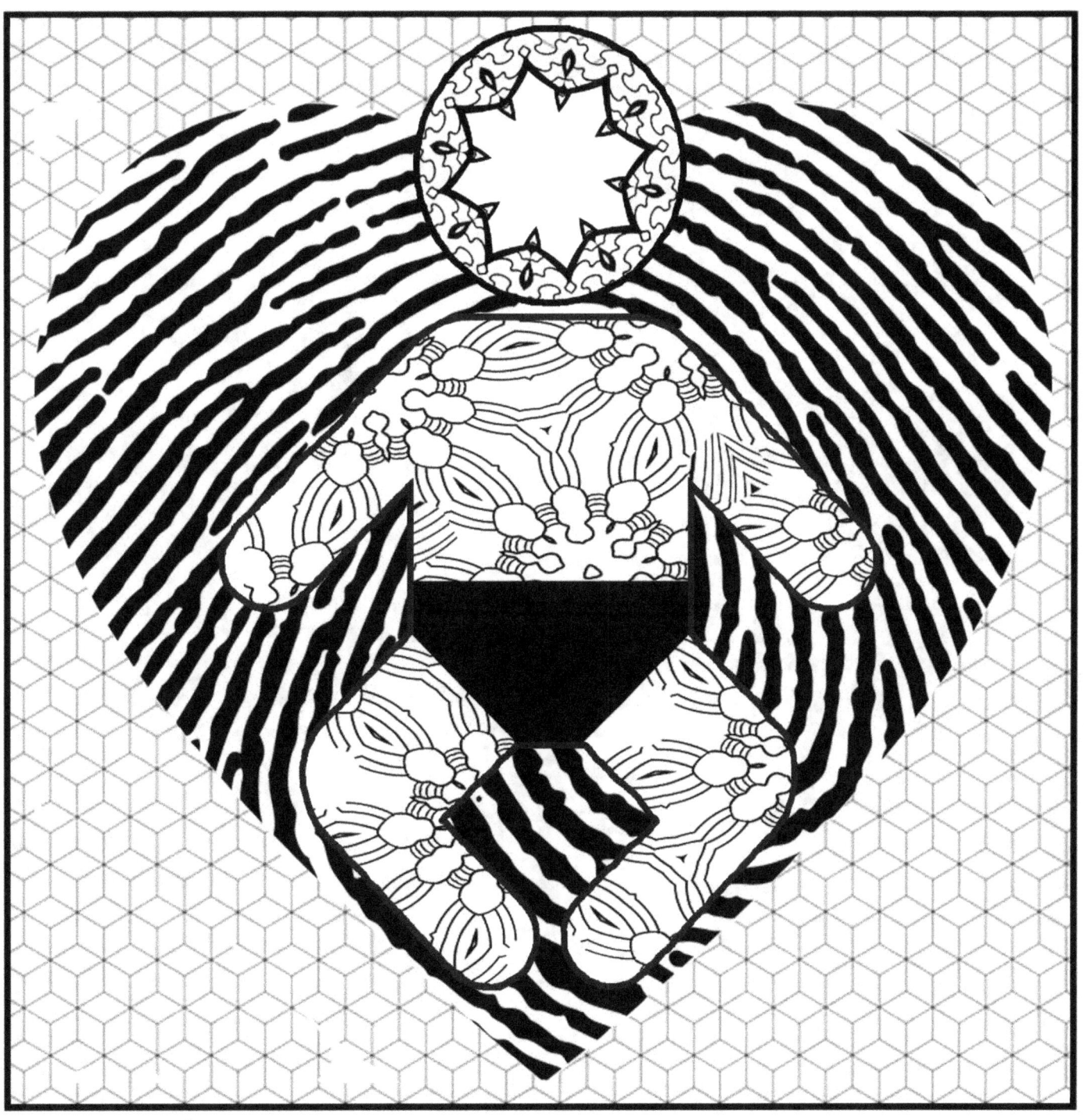

33. CLOTH DIAPER PIN

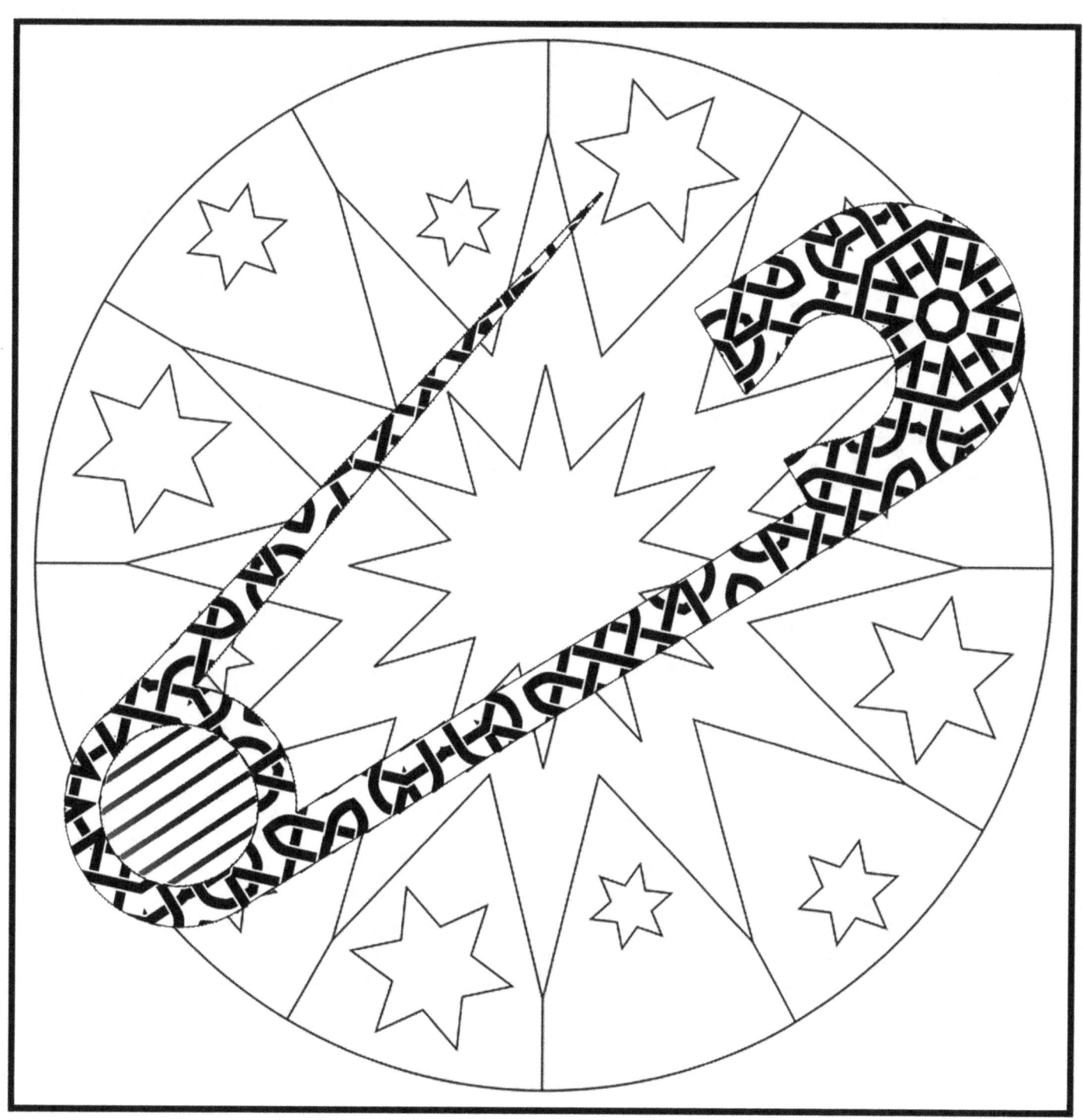

34. BABY IN STROLLER

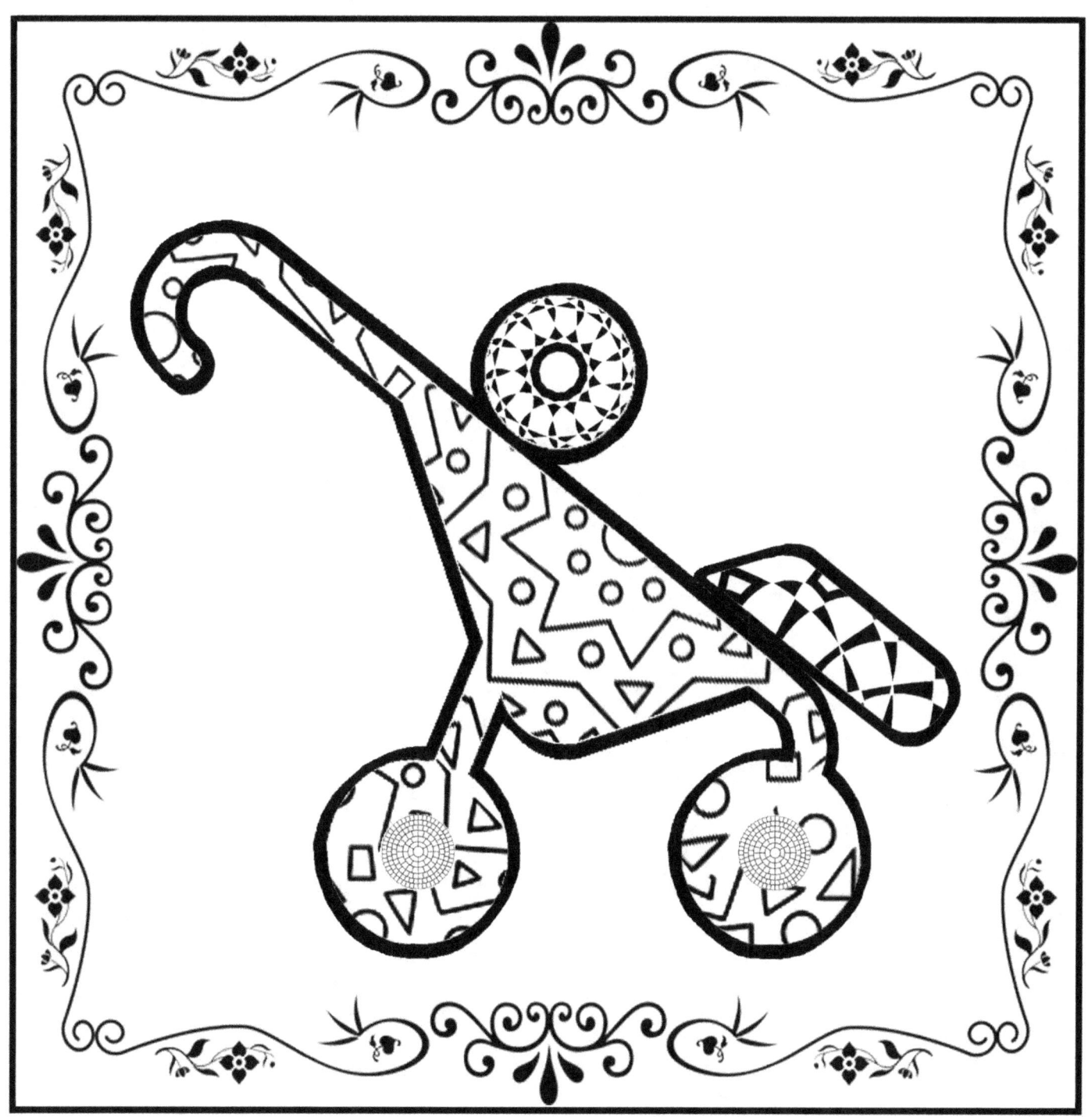

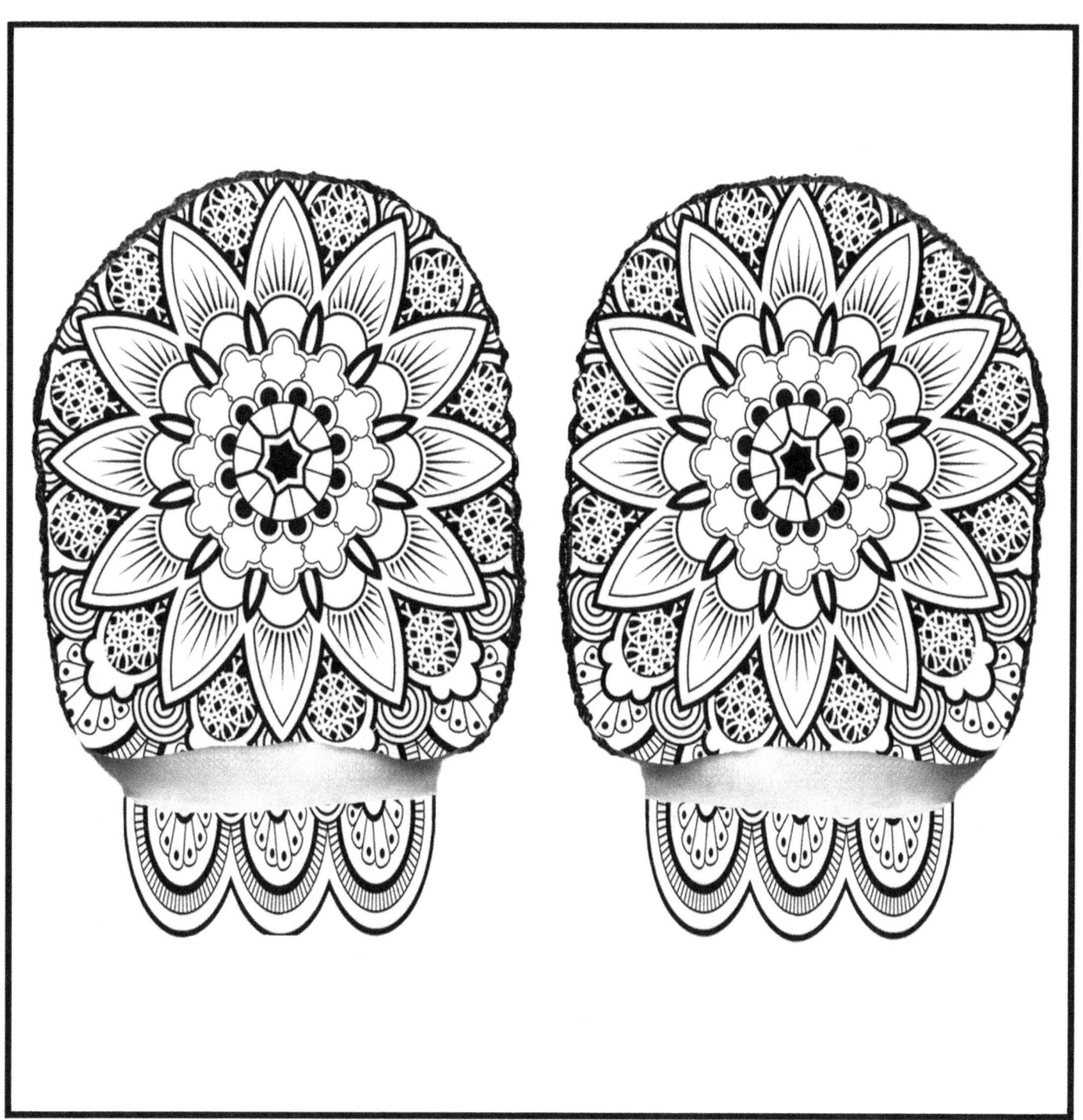

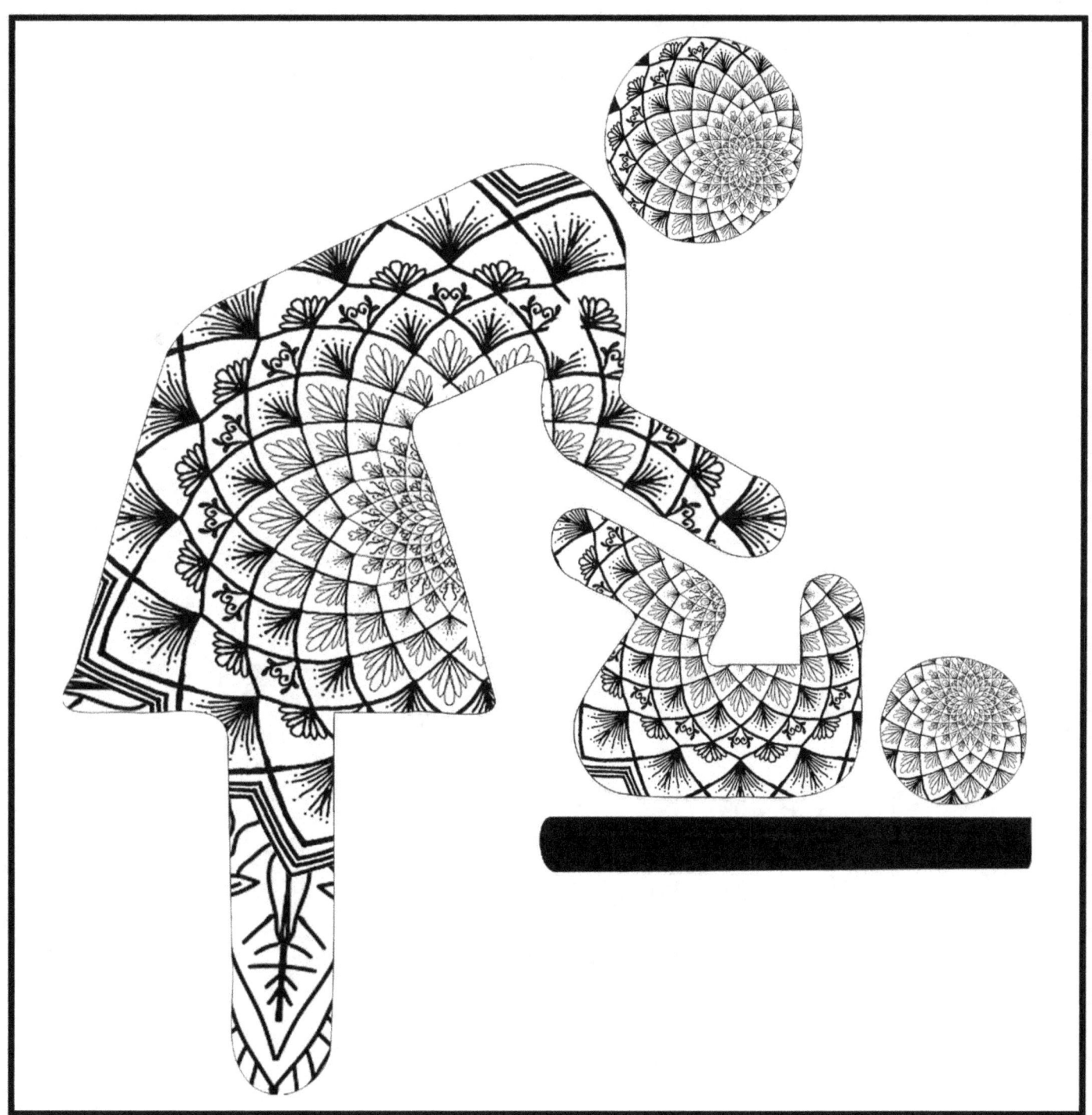

37. CRAWLING BABY

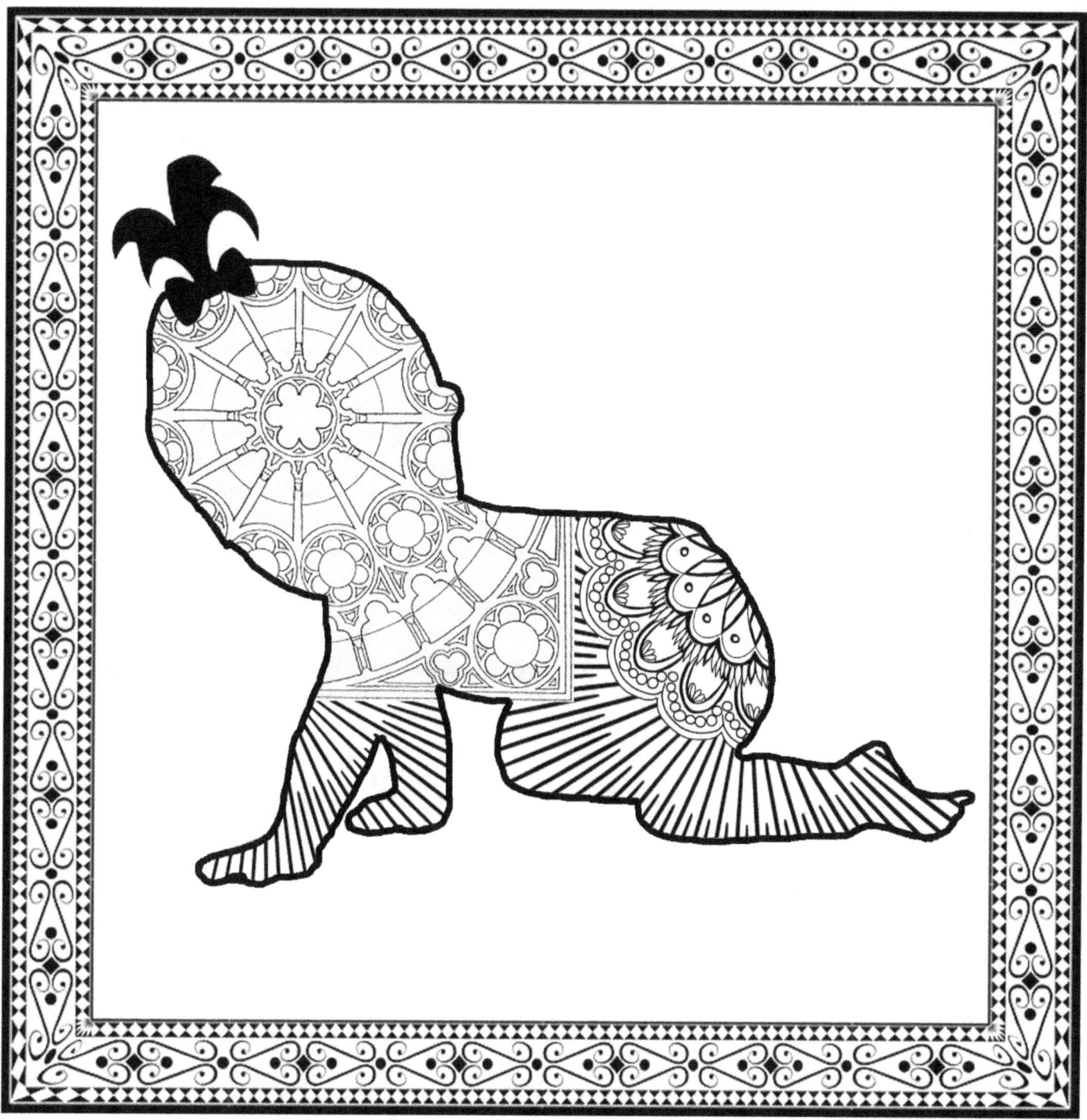

38. CROCHET BABY BOOTIE

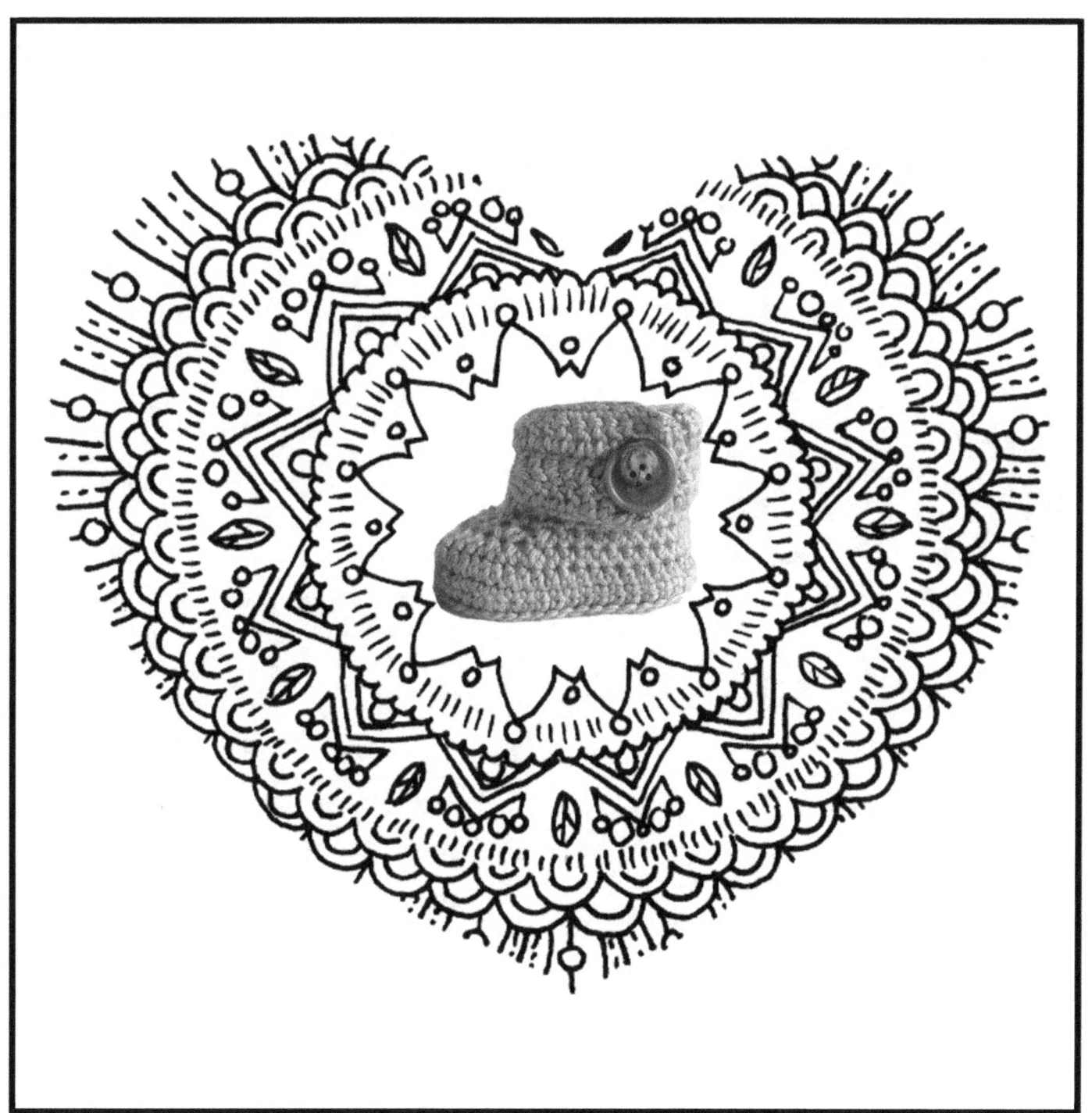

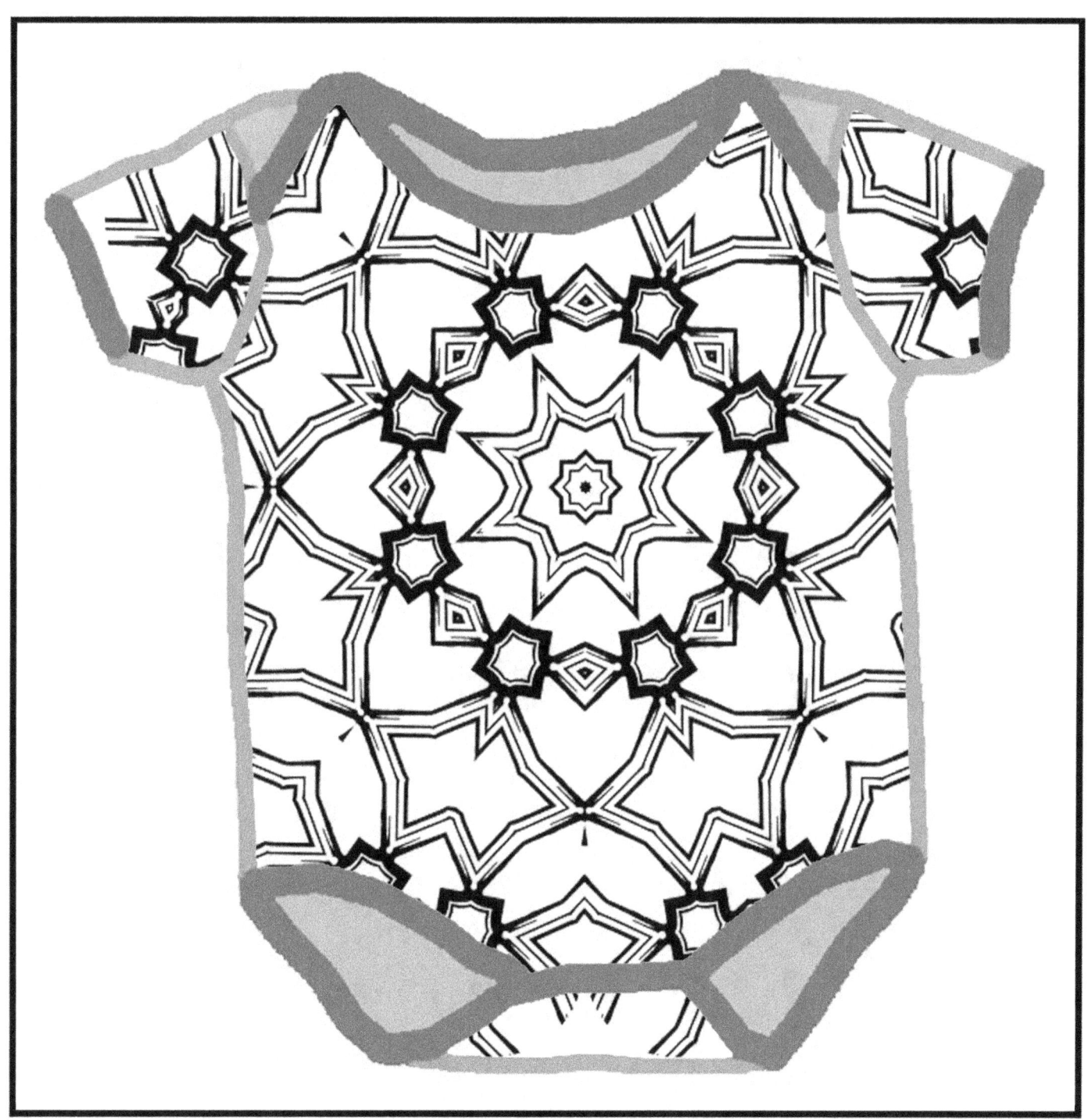

40. BABY WITH TEDDY AND BLANKET

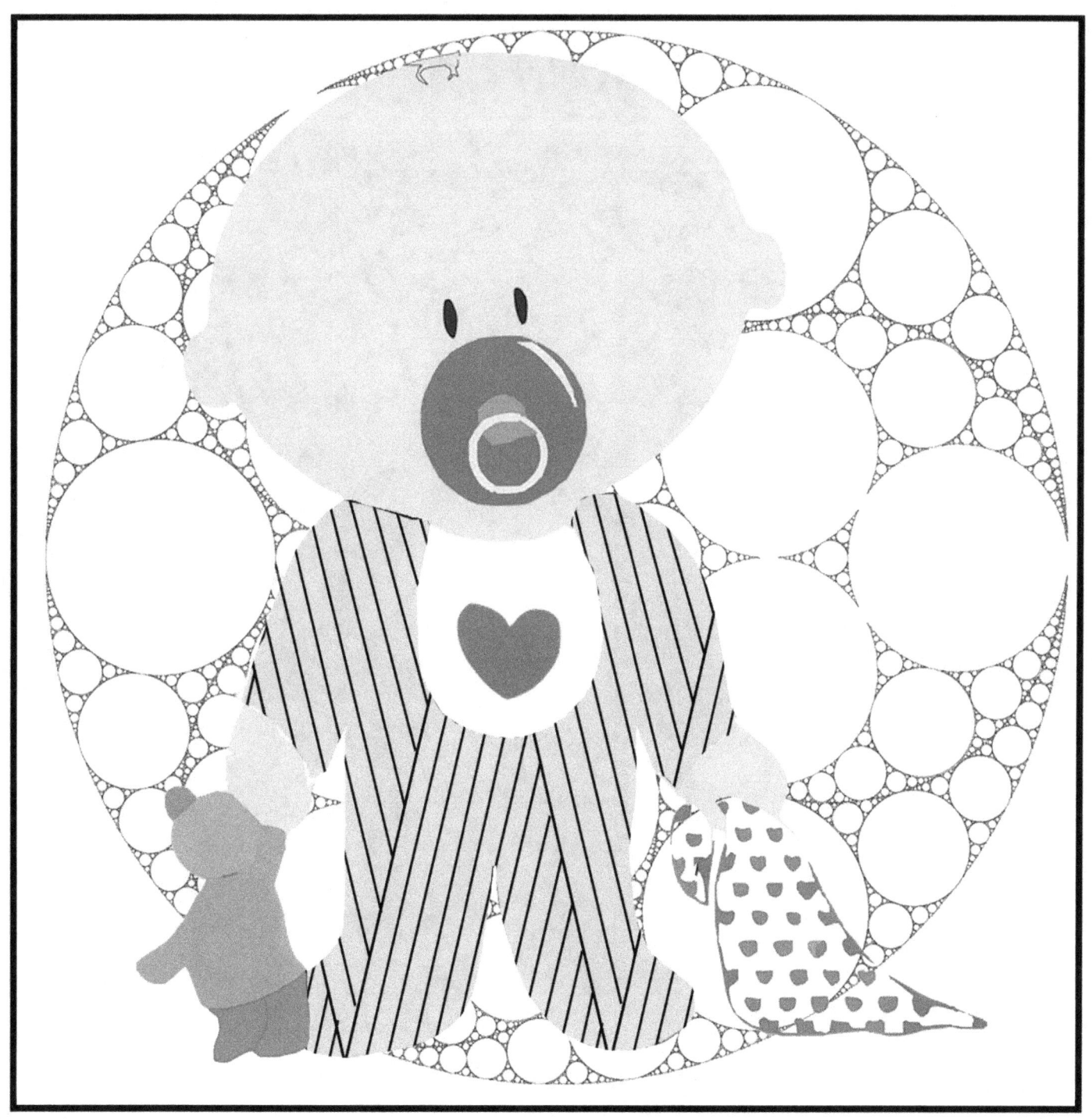

41. ULTRASOUND IMAGE

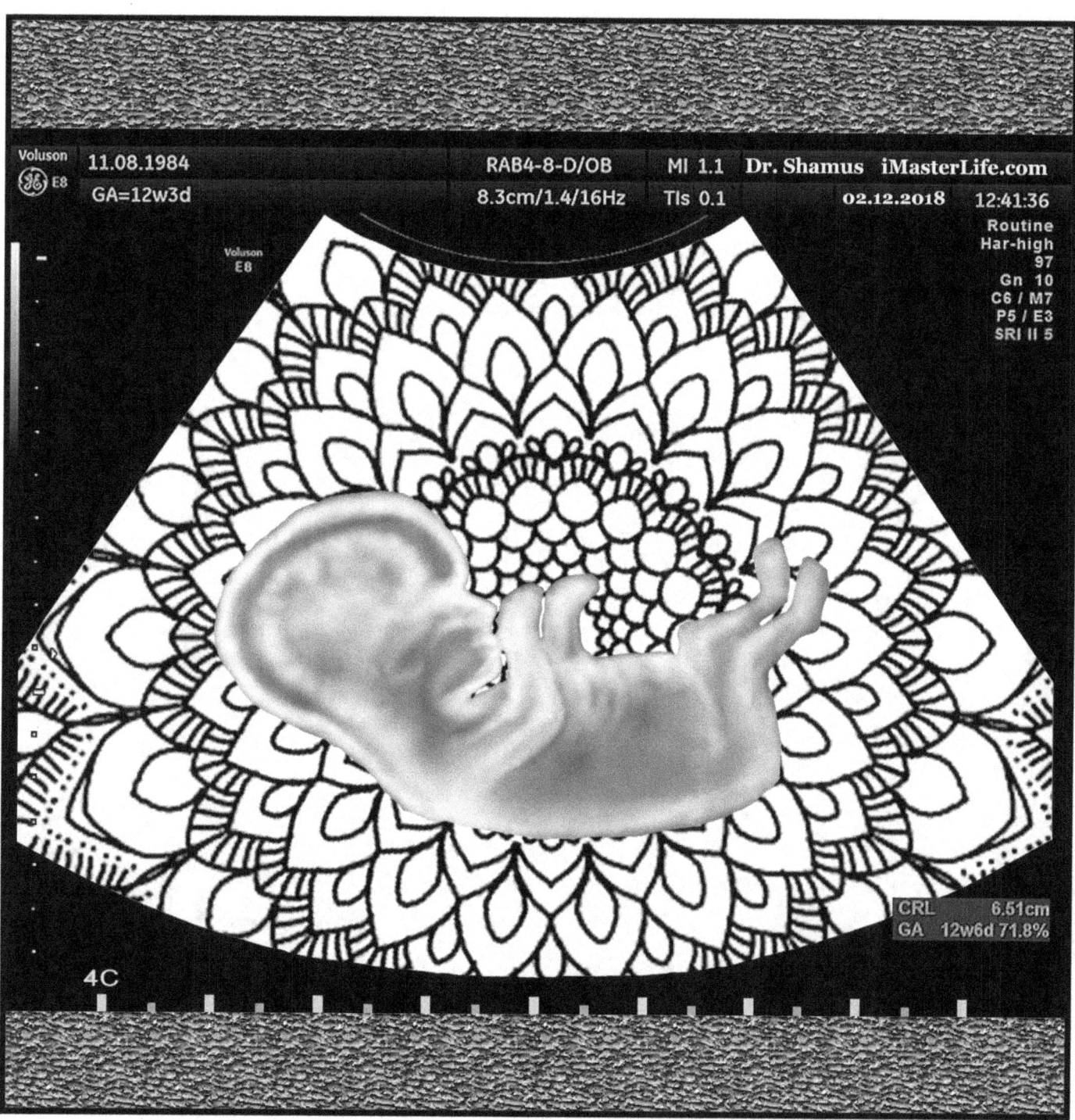

42. Swaddled Baby

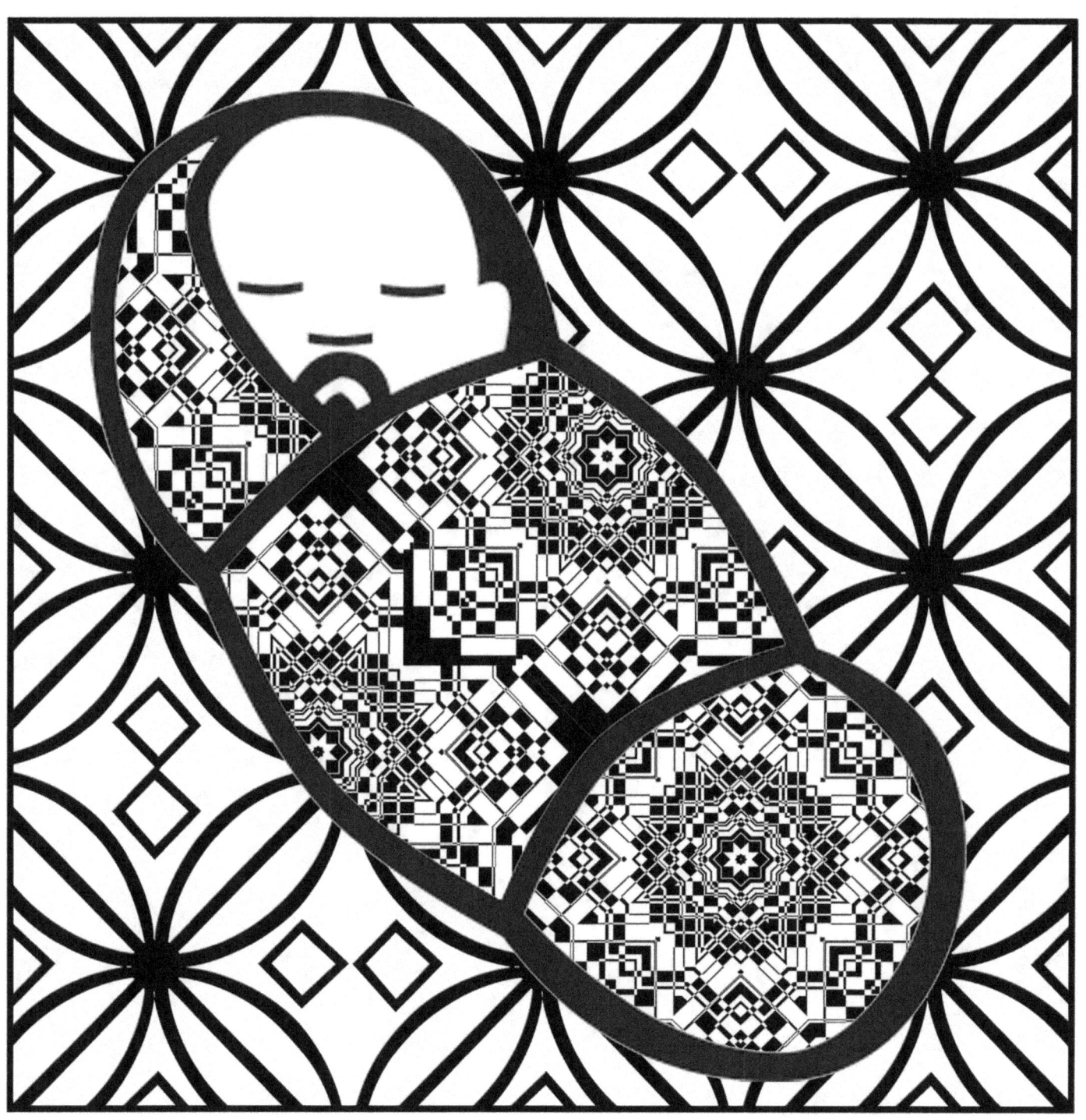

43. Mommy Lifting Baby

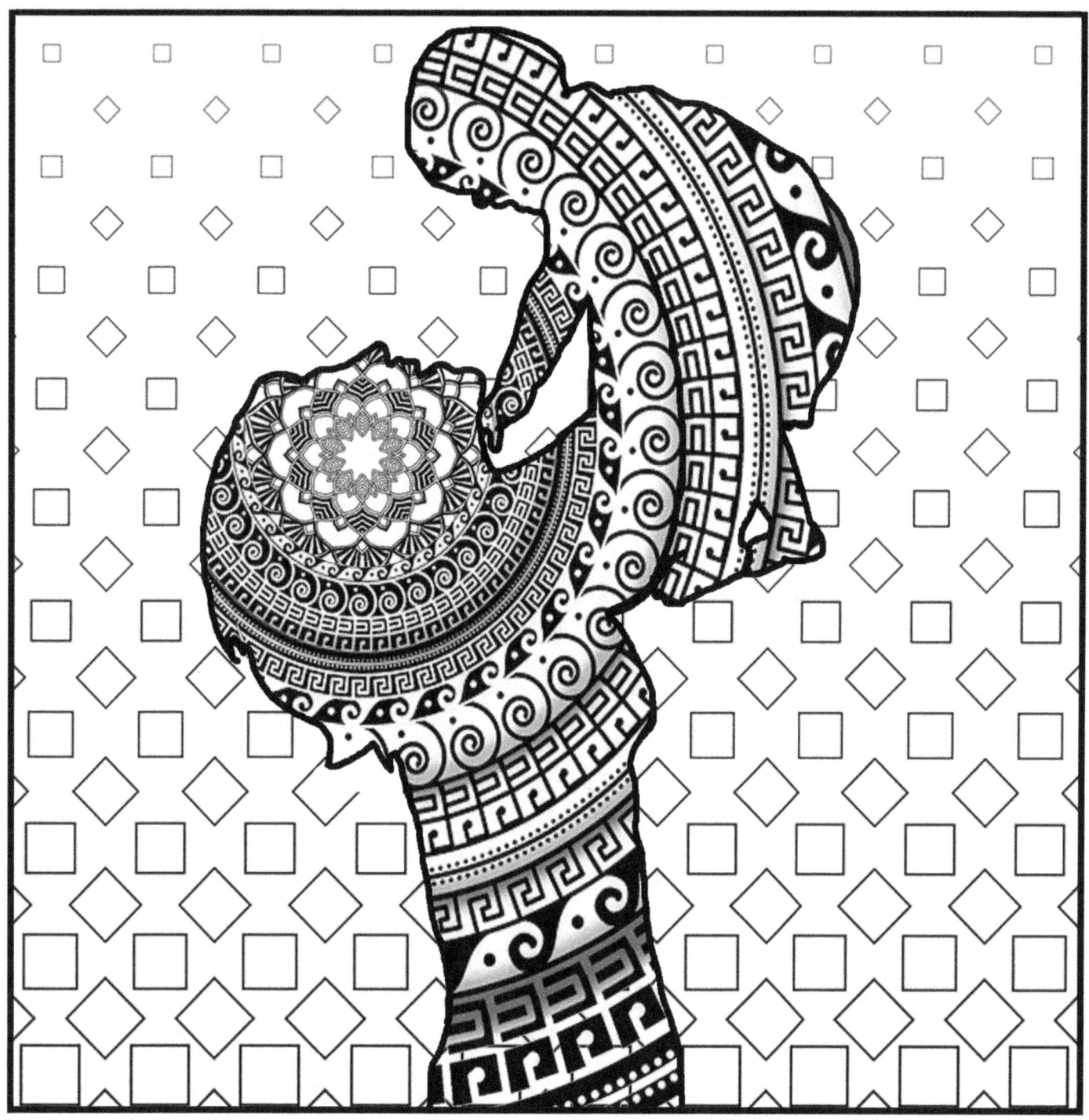

44. SLEEPING BABY IN MANGER

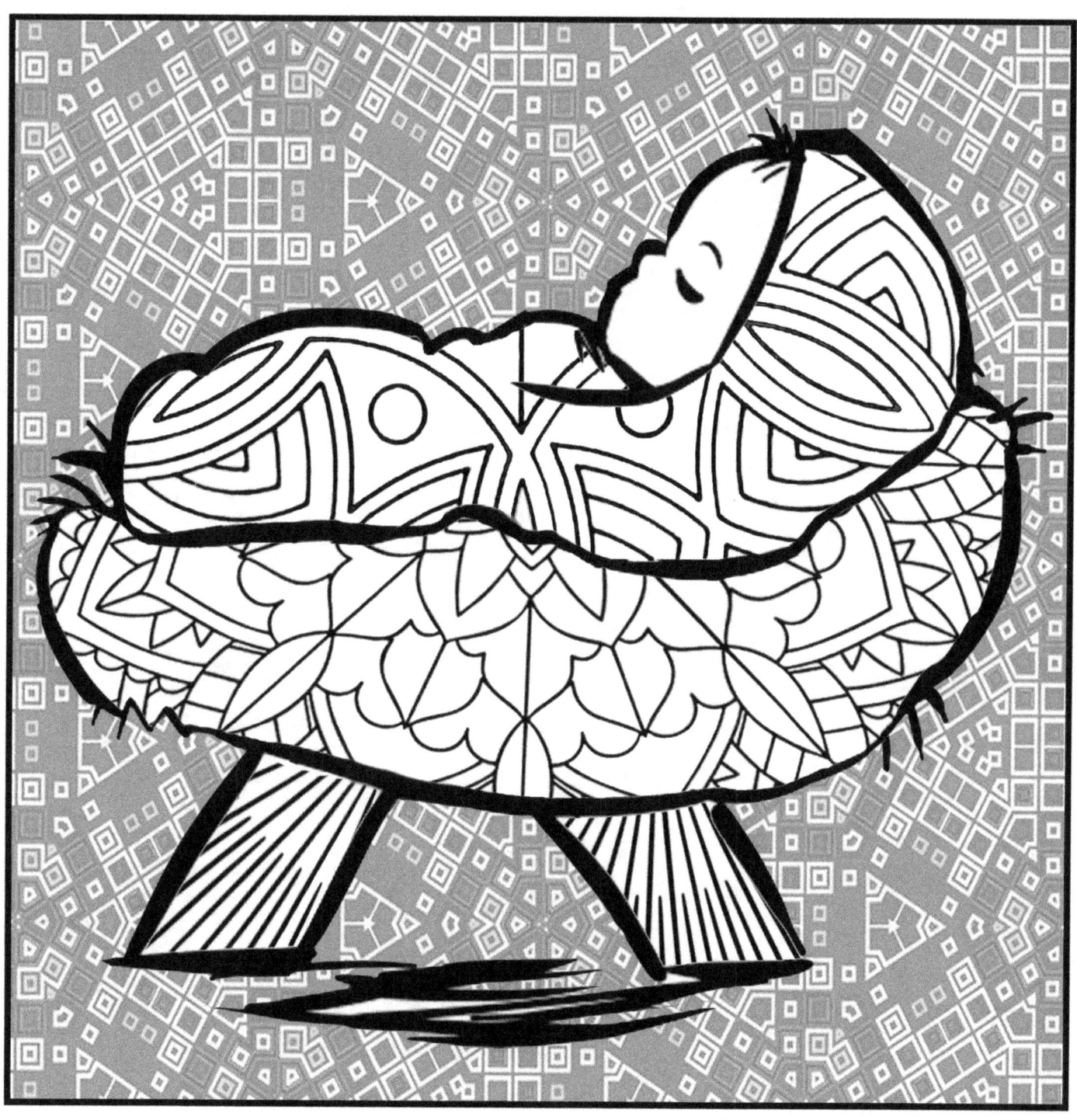

45. Baby Face

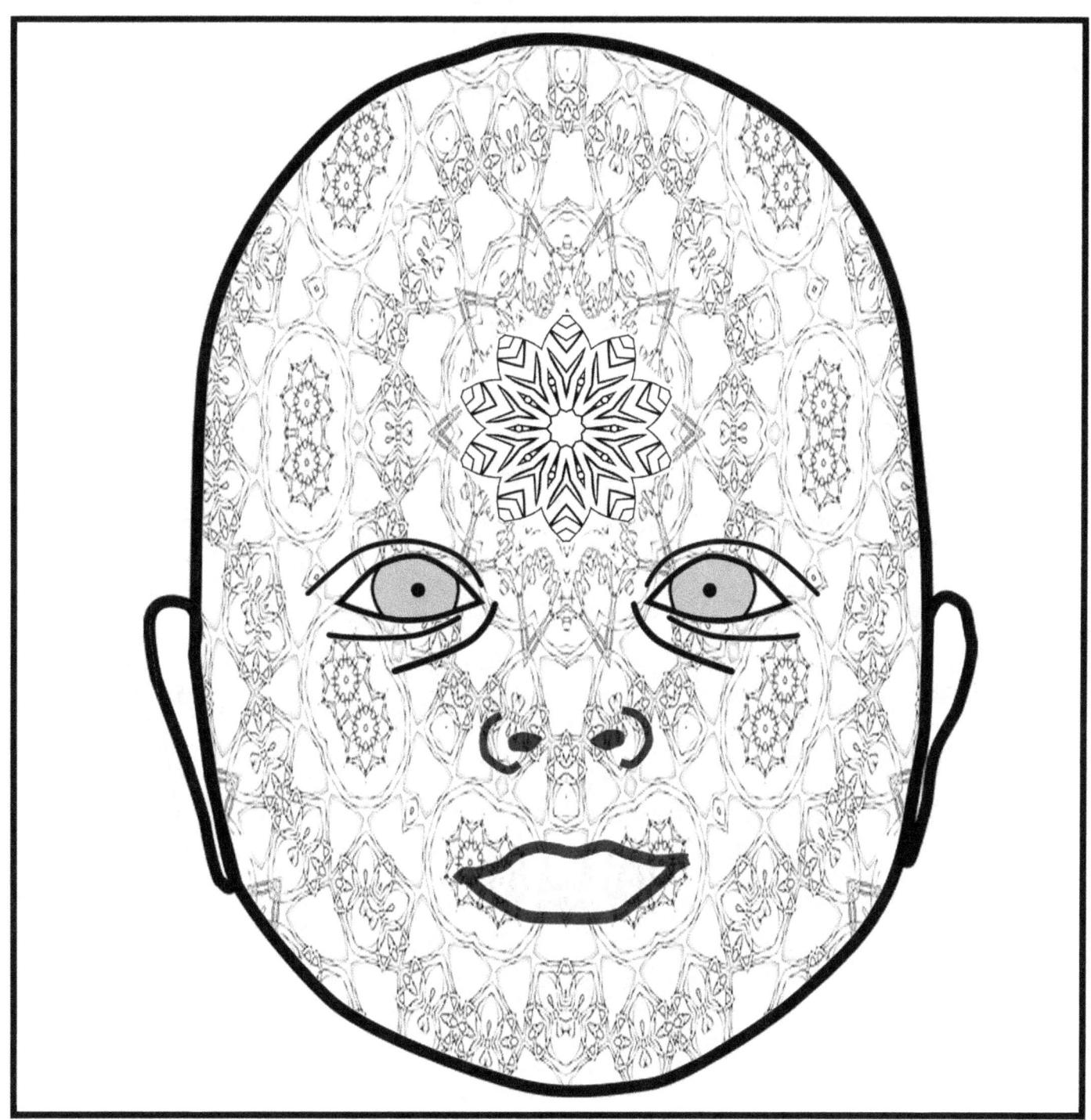

46. BABY BOTTLE

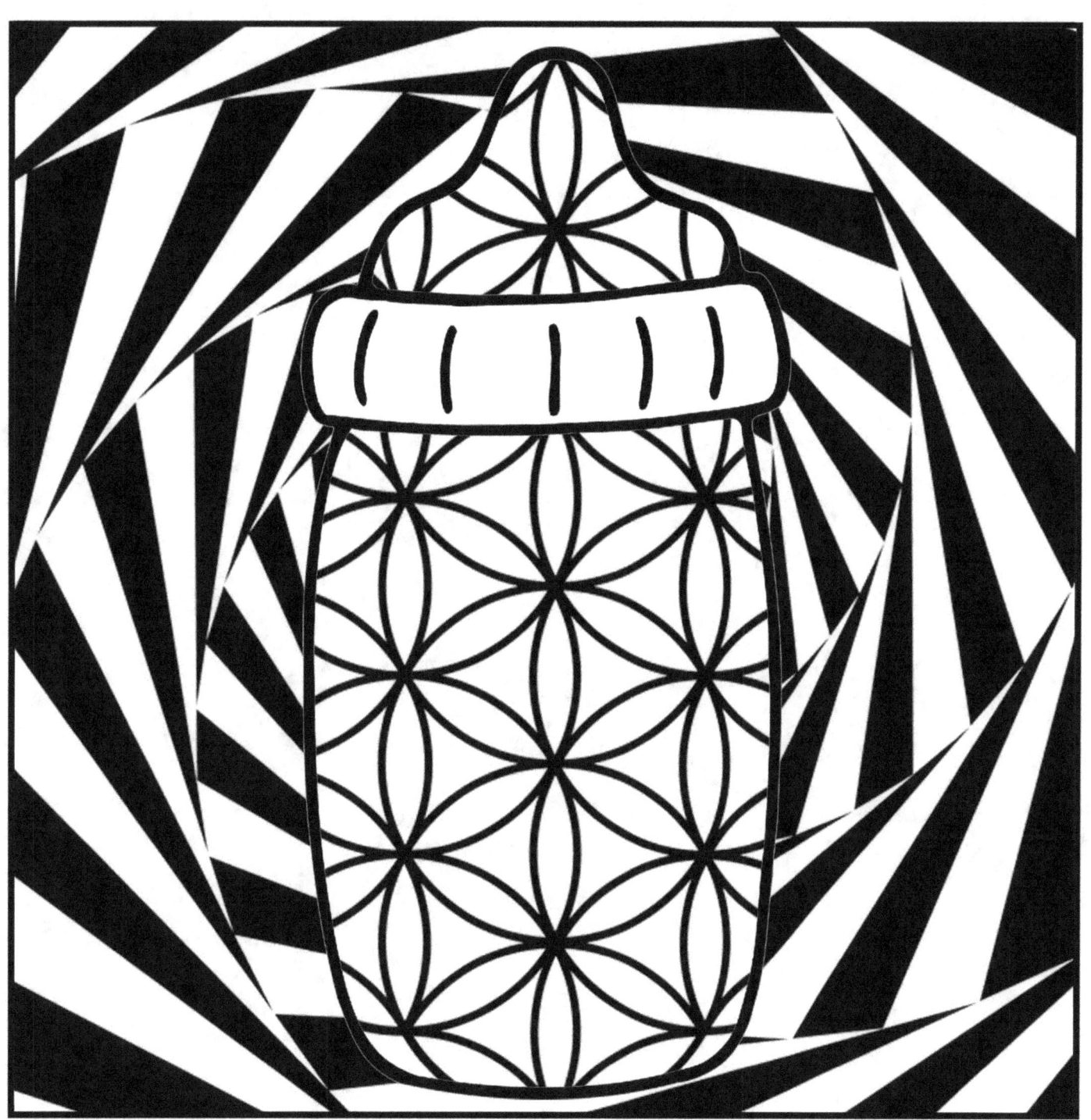

47. Baby Carriage

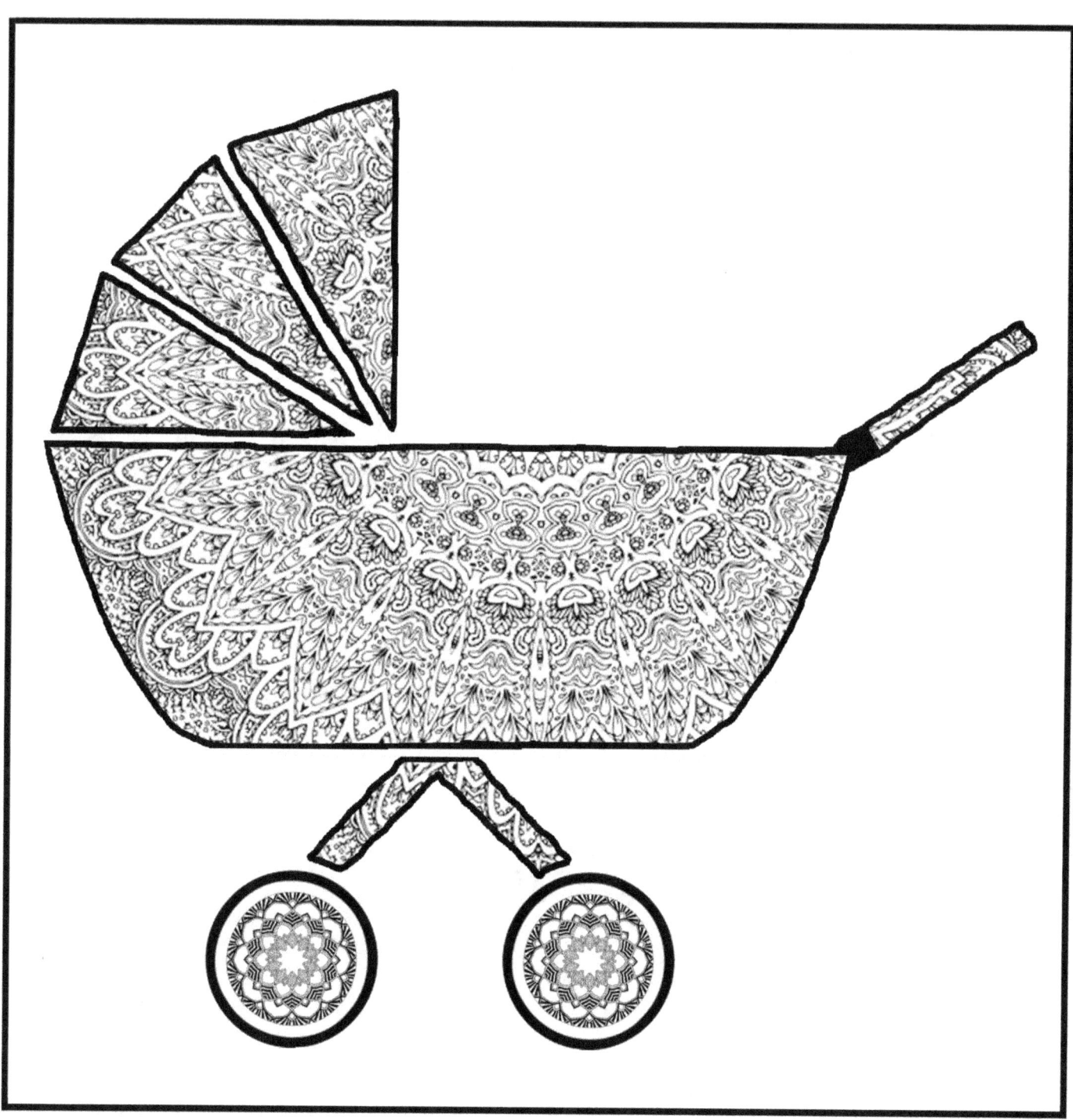

48. POSITIVE PREGNANCY TEST

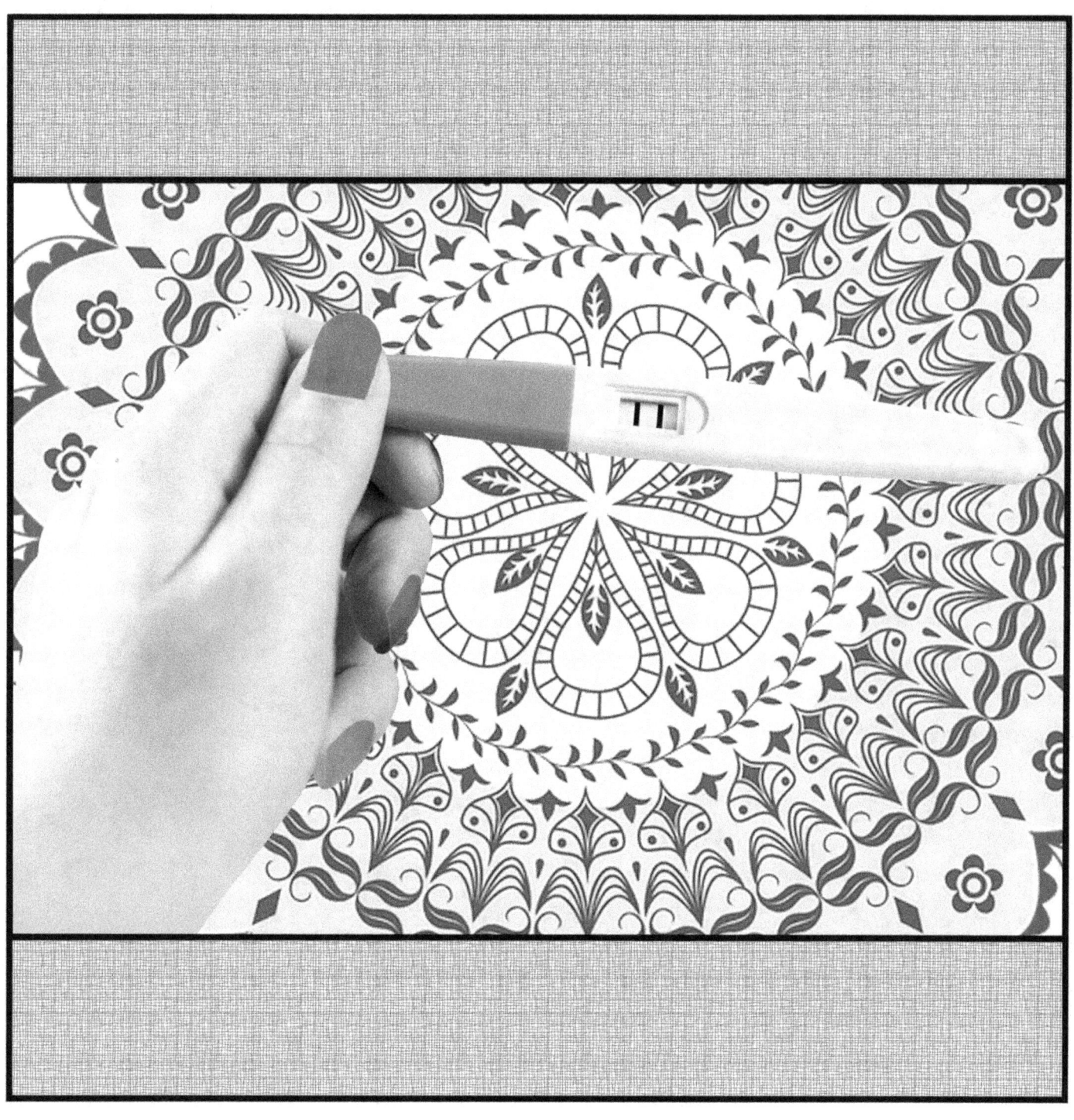

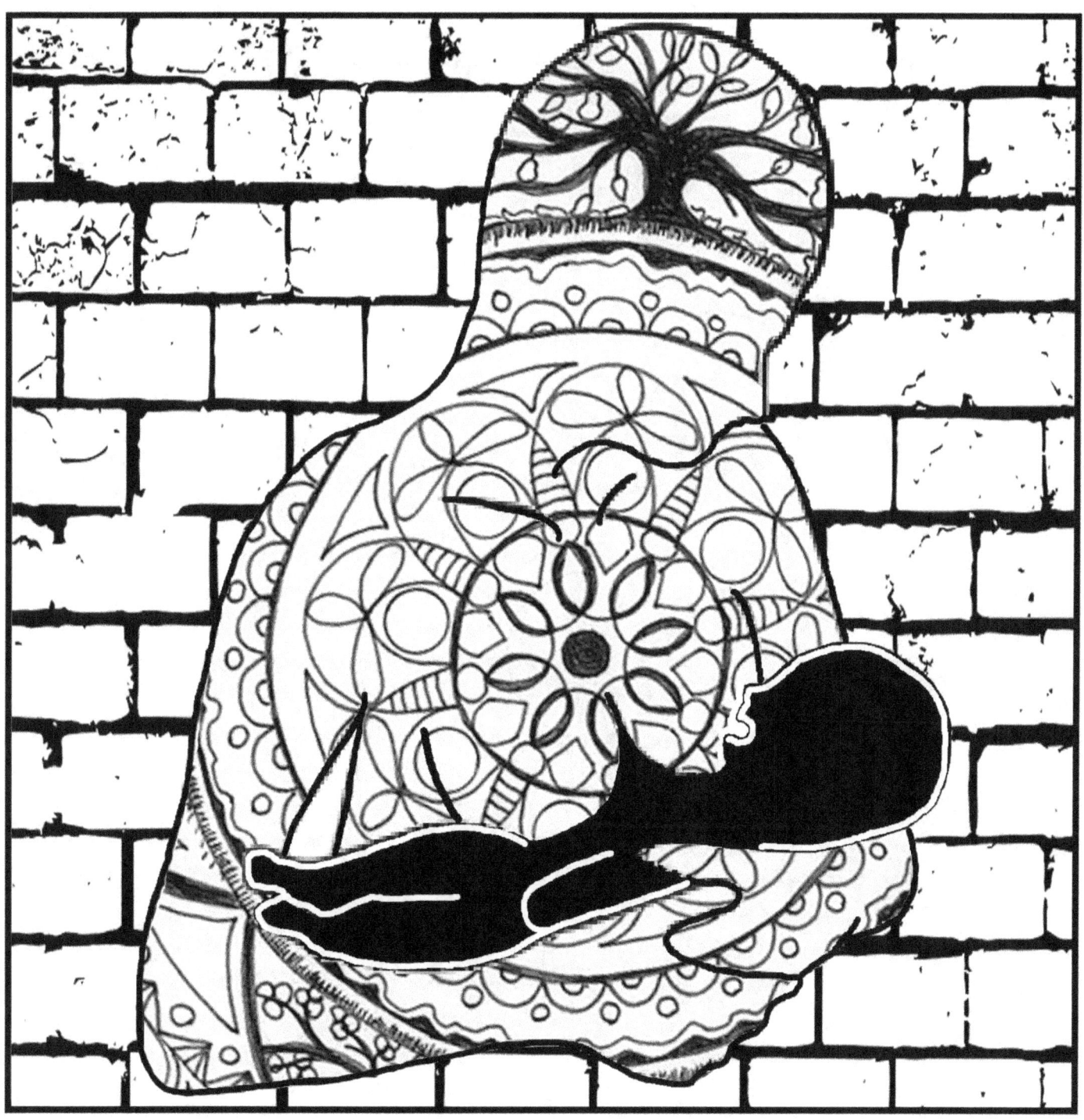

50. BABY'S FIRST STEP

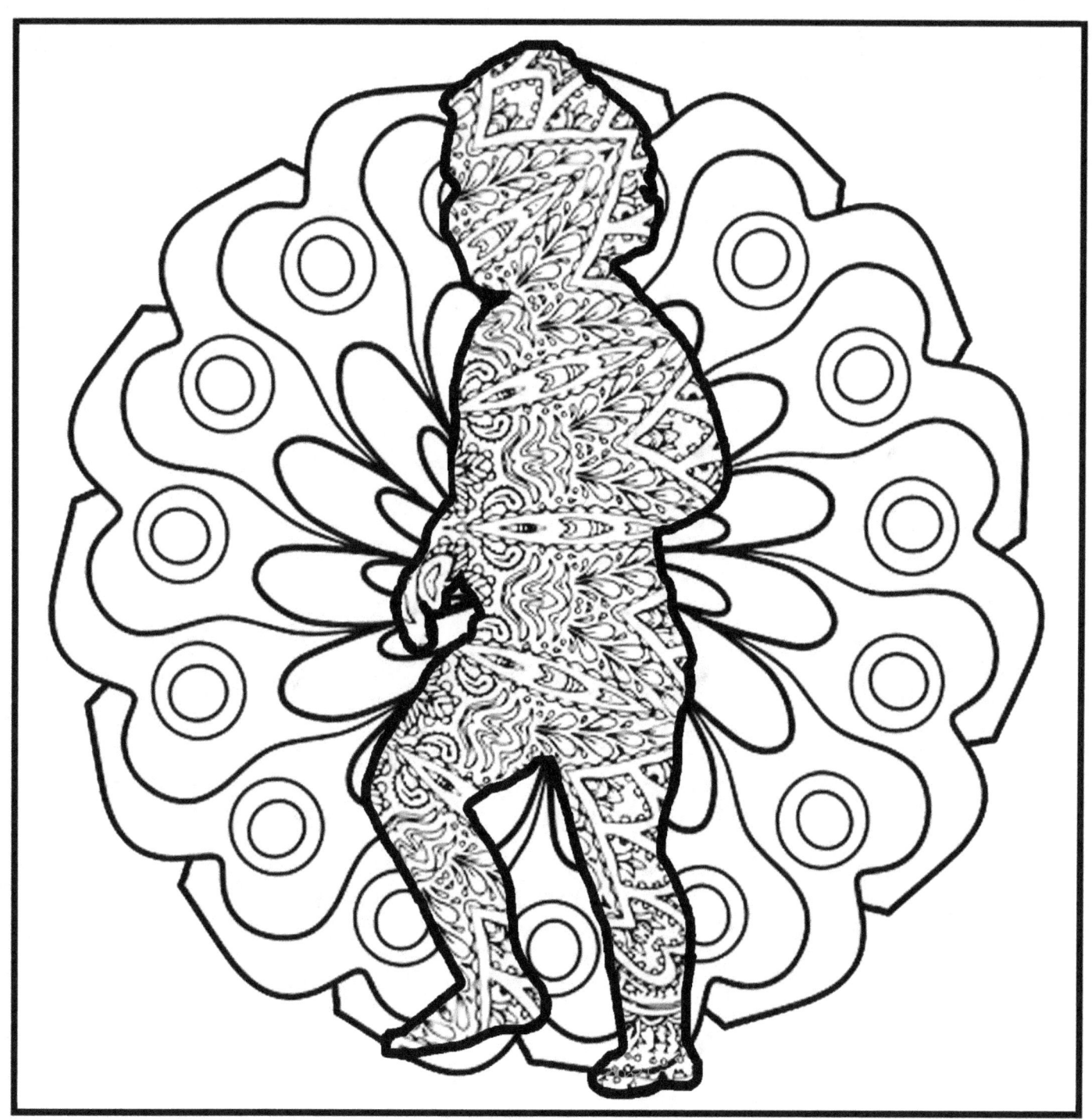

51. Rubber Ducky

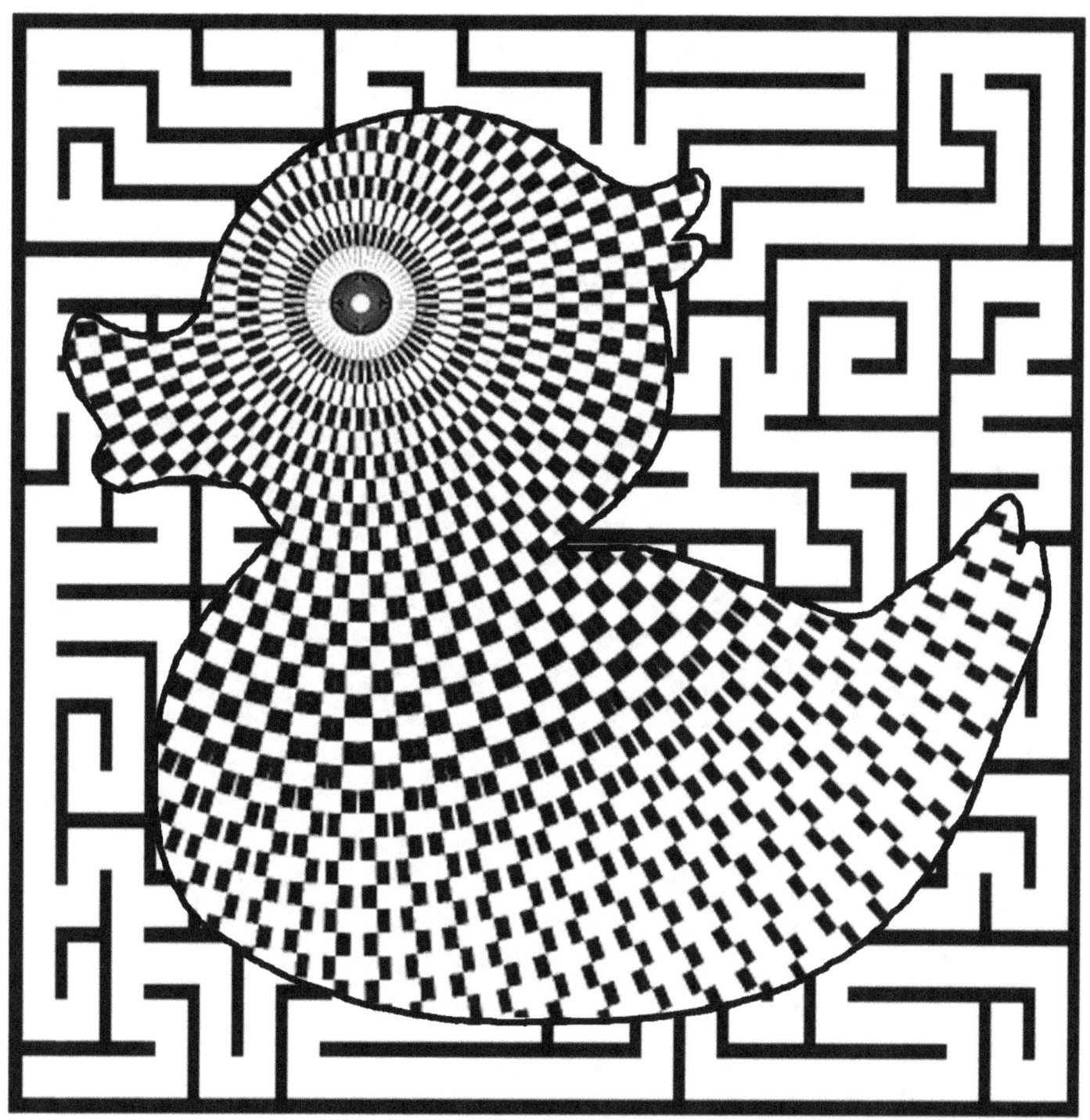

52. Baby Wooden Block

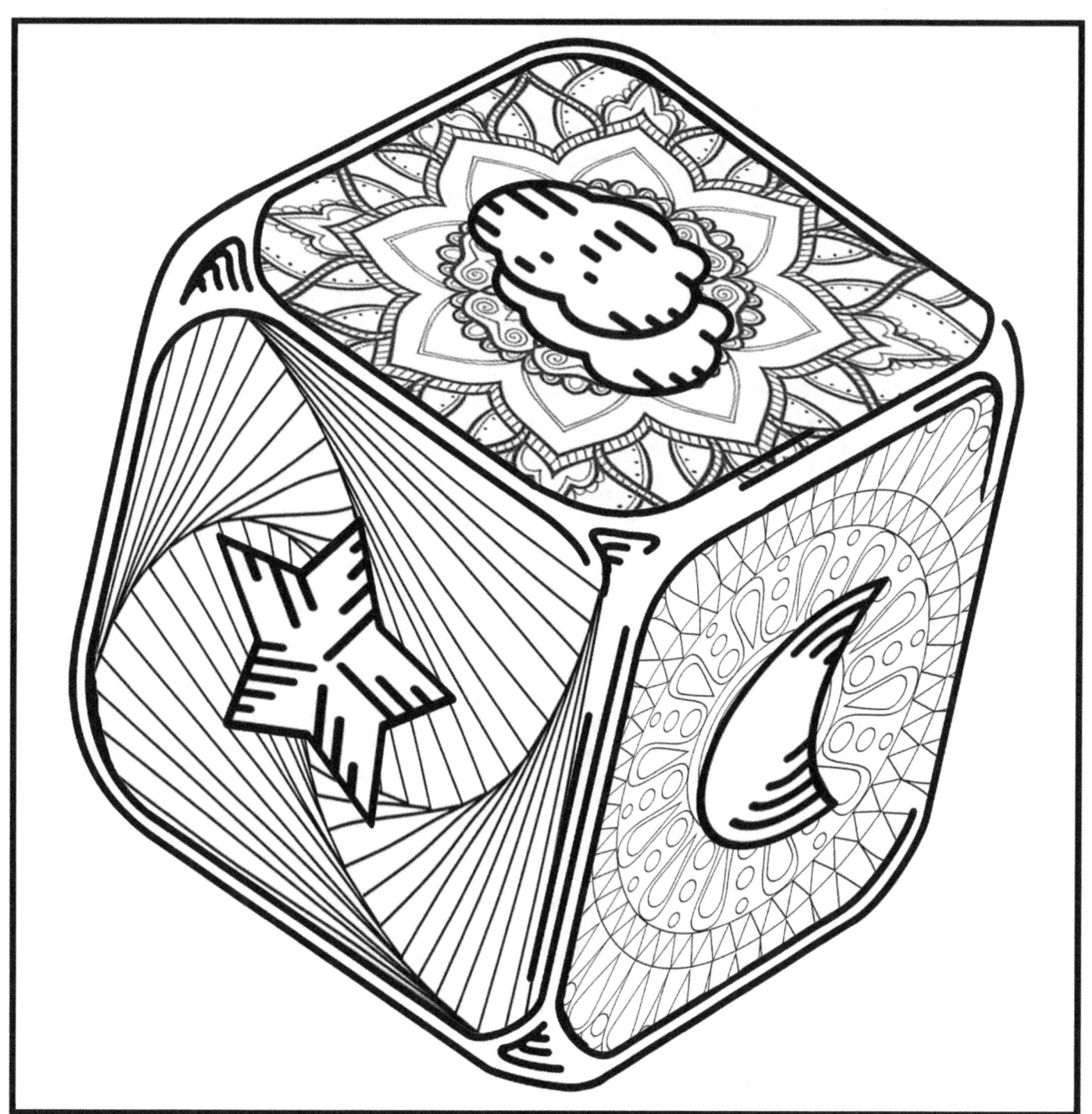

CLOSING

We hope you had as much fun coloring each of the pages in this book as Marc & I did in putting all 52 Mandala style illustrations together. We want to end this book with a poem I wrote for my children. May it bring warmth and blessings to you and your family too.

Thank You!

Silvia Shamus & Marc Shamus

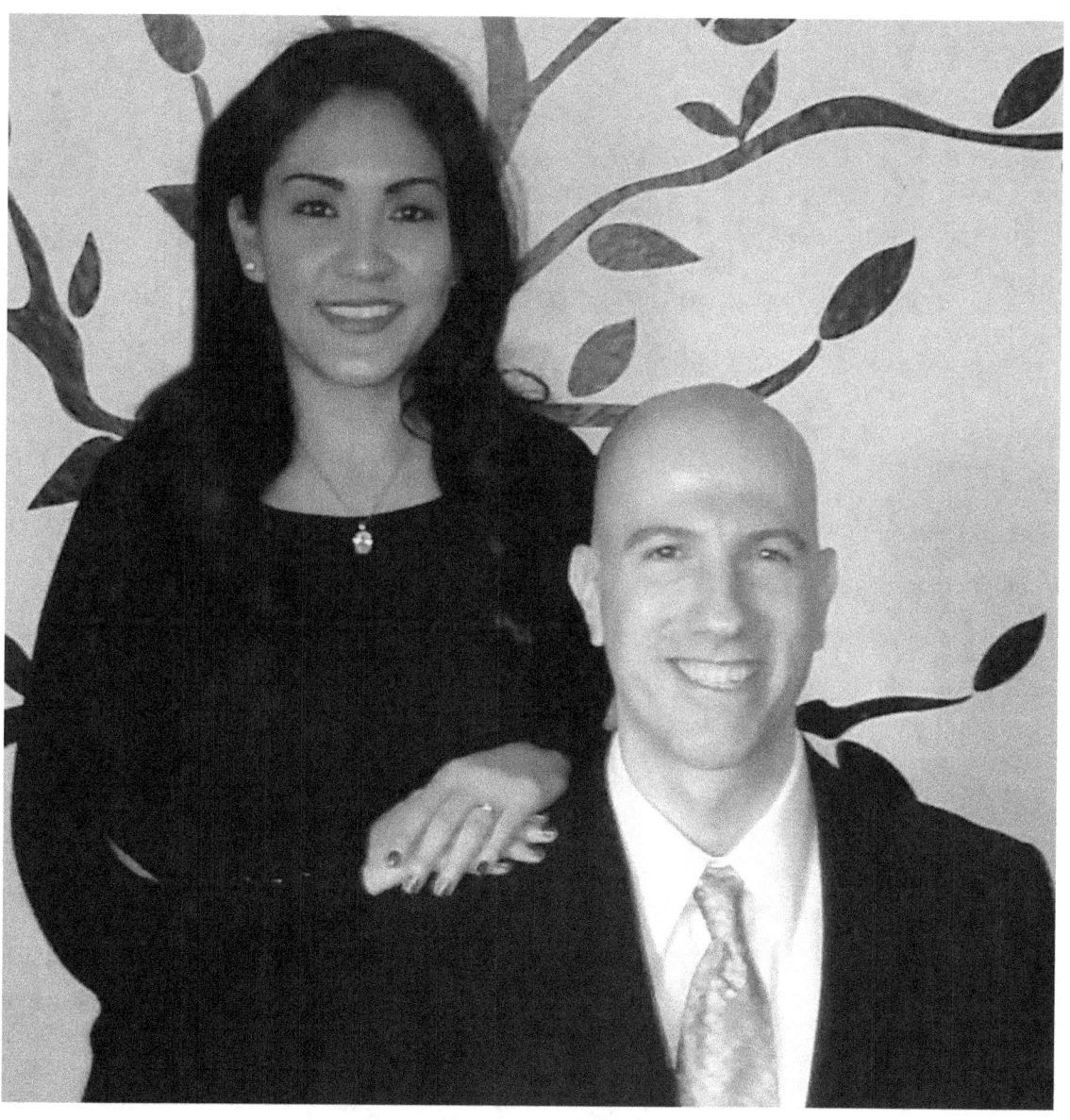

Silvia Shamus & Marc Shamus

SAFE IN MY ARMS by Silvia Shamus

~for my children (Kuki, Kali, Zivena, Kimiko and Zen)

I will keep you
Safe in my arms
Just as I'll always
Keep you inside my heart

When you are small
I will hold you
So close to me
To ensure you do not fall

And when you get hurt
I will kiss the ouchies away
I will provide you comfort
And take away your pain.

As you start to grow
I will give you space to explore
To become your own person
Flourishing you with love and adoration

When you are ready to fly with your own wings
No one will cheer you more than I
To see you fly high in the sky day and night
As you pursue your inspiring dreams

And even when you are grown
I will be there for you
For you won't be on your own
I will always be there too

110

In the sunshine

In the snow

In the stormy weather

In the dampness of fog

I will be there with you

I will keep you protected

Safe in my arms

Safe in my arms you will always be

Close in my heart to never leave

You can be sure you'll remain intact

Here with my sweet memories

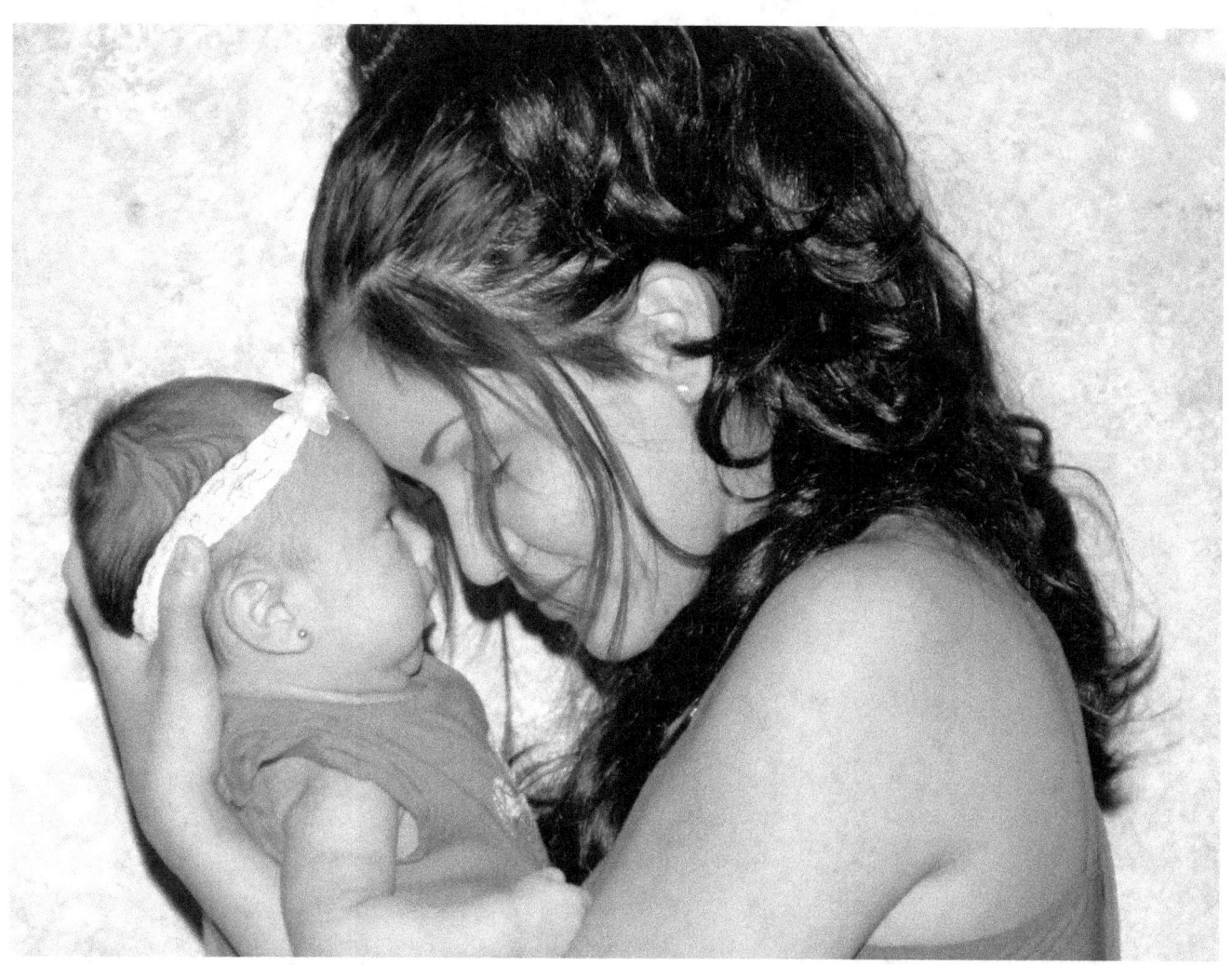

Silvia Shamus in January 2005 with First Baby Kuki Shamus

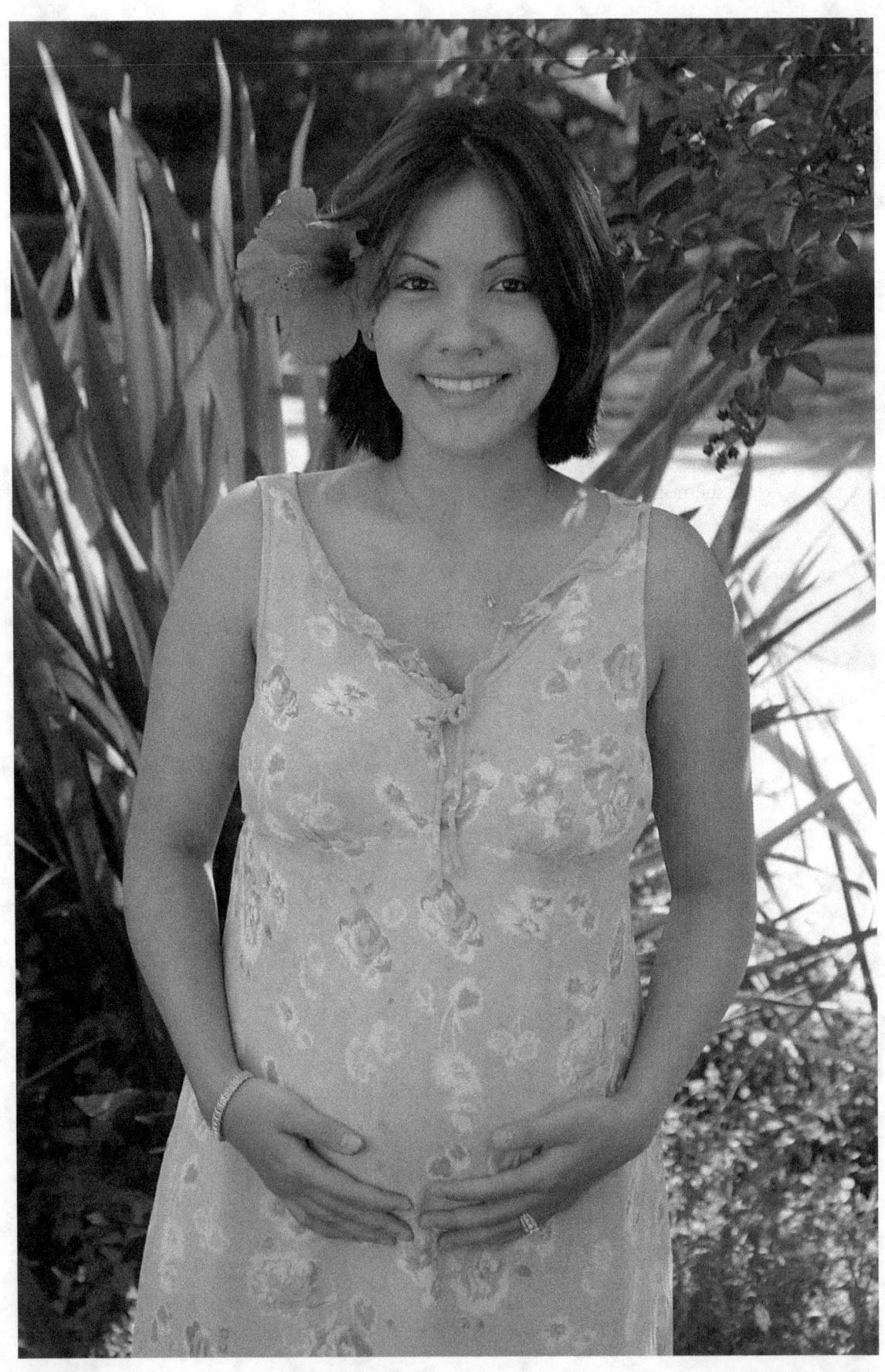

Silvia Shamus in September 2004 Pregnant with First Baby

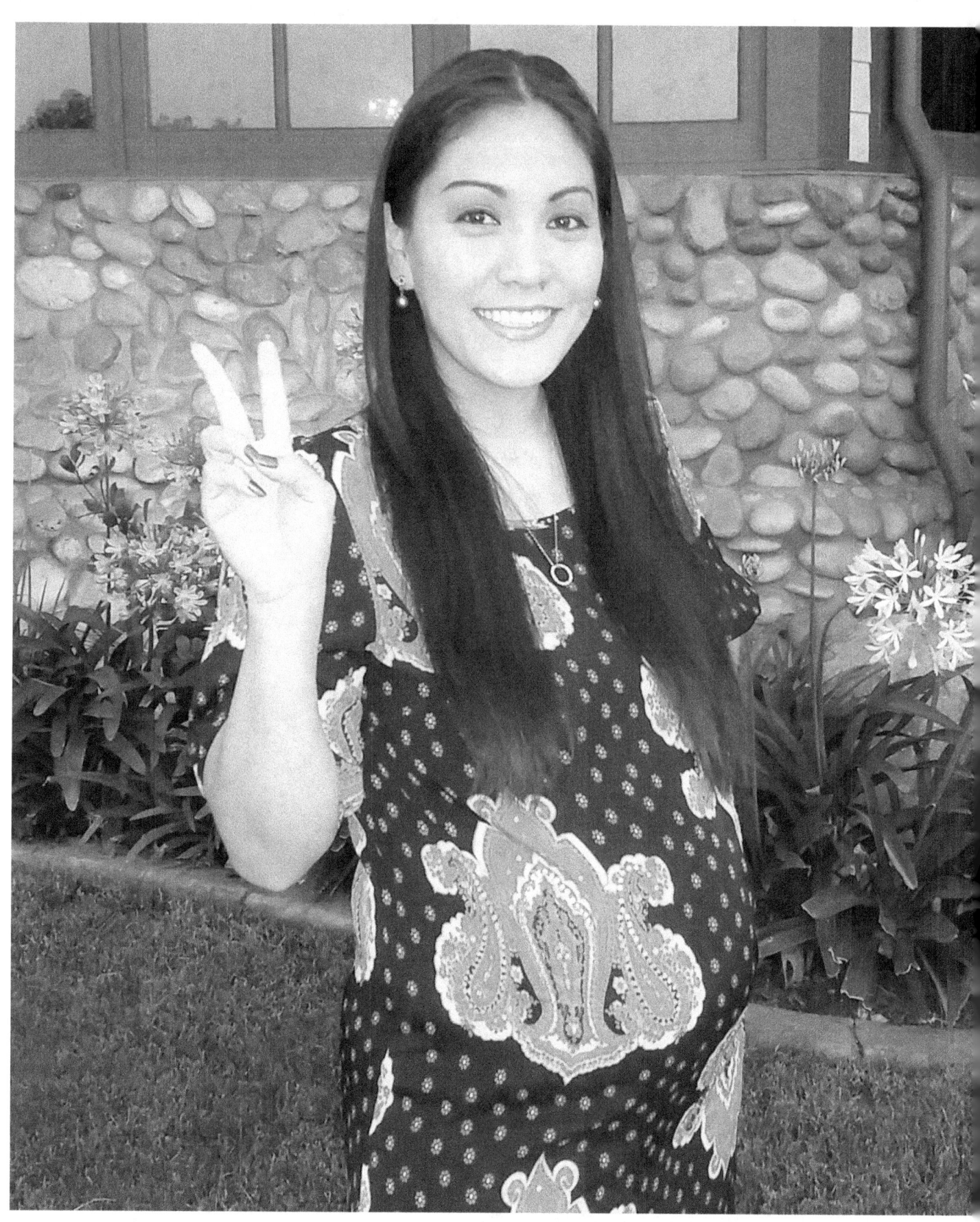

Silvia Shamus in May 2015 Pregnant with Fifth Baby

ABOUT THE AUTHOR – SILVIA SHAMUS

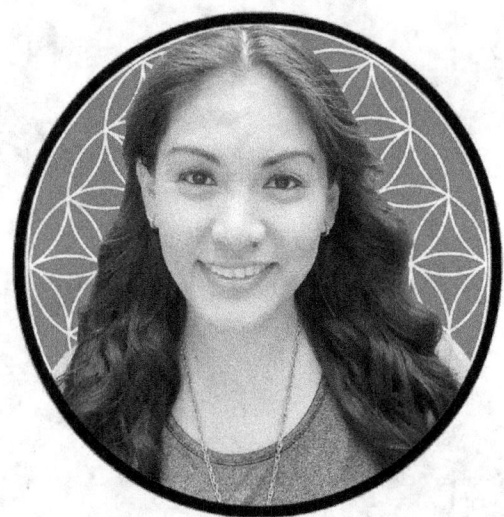

Silvia Shamus is a lifelong lover of health and wellness. She has a background as an entrepreneur and homemaker. She loves educating and inspiring others to live a life filled with vigor.

Learn more about Silvia at:

iMasterLife.com/SilviaShamus

ABOUT THE AUTHOR – MARC SHAMUS

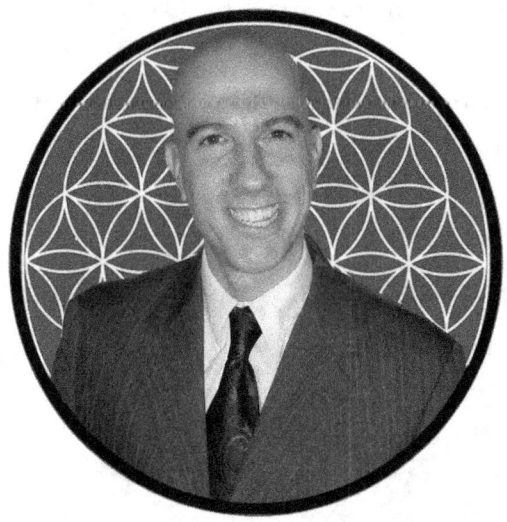

Marc Shamus is a teacher of life strategies and ideas that may improve the quality of the people's lives. He is a Published Author, Life Educator, Public Speaker and Entrepreneur.

Learn more about Marc at:

iMasterLife.com/MarcShamus

Learn more about Marc's Publishing Company at:

iMasterLife.com

Personal Dedication

This book is dedicated to our five children who have blessed our lives in infinite ways. WE LOVE YOU!

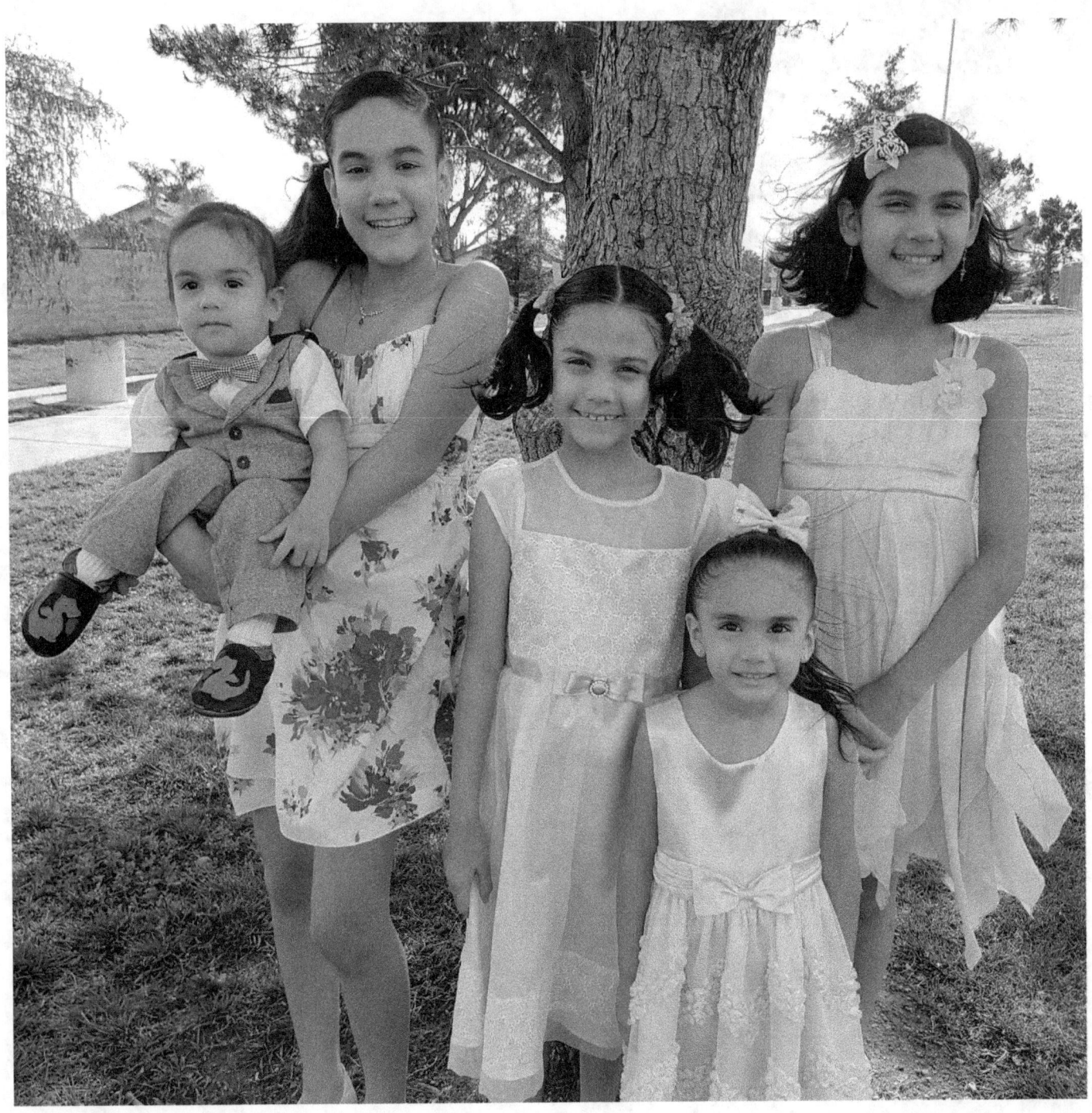

Zen Shamus, Kuki Shamus, Zivena Shamus, Kimiko Shamus & Kali Shamus

DID YOU LOVE PREGNANCY COLORING BOOK FOR ADULTS?

Thank you for investing in yourself and in this book.

If you enjoyed this book, please let others know how much they can benefit from it by leaving a review here:

iMasterLife.com/Reviews/Silvia2

If you have feedback on how to make this book even better, I'd love to hear it at **info@imasterlife.com**

Thanks!

Marc Shamus

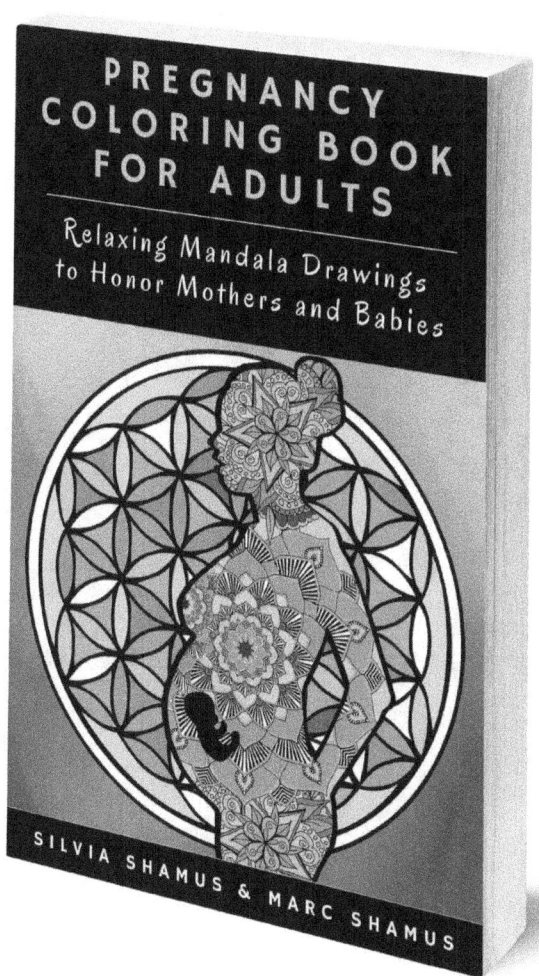

Thanks again for your support!

RECOMMENDED PUBLICATIONS

Go to:

iMasterLife.com/hobby

WATCH OUR VIDEO COURSES

Get access to training video courses by going to **iMasterLife.com/Courses**

Inside these course, you'll discover...

• **What are the <u>Basics</u> of each taught subject**

• **How to <u>Make</u> <u>Your</u> <u>Life</u> <u>Better</u> as you learn & apply lessons**

• **How <u>Powerful</u> "YOU" really are**

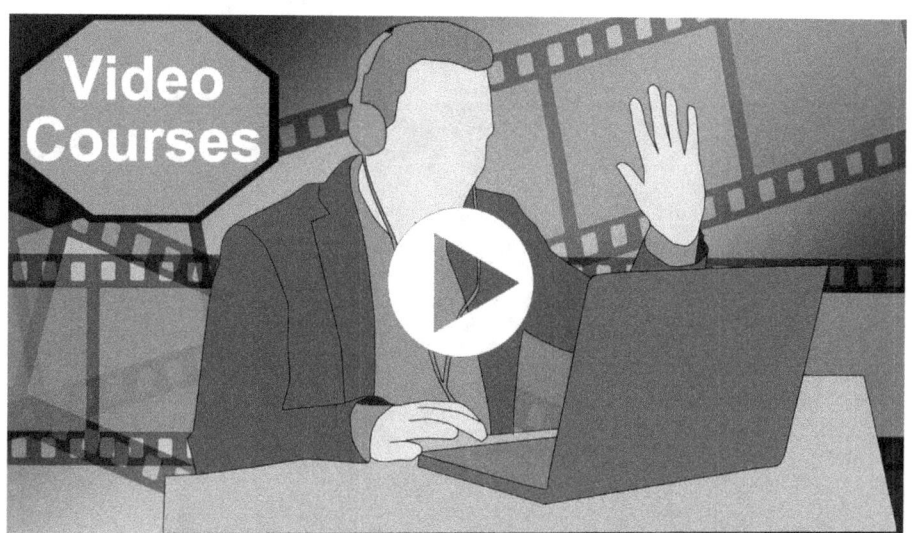

iMasterLife.com/Courses

www.ingramcontent.com/pod-product-compliance
Lightning Source LLC
Chambersburg PA
CBHW081729220526
45468CB00008B/2034